INDEPENDENT WRITING

Second Edition

Teresa D. O'Donnell
TESOL Central Office

Judith L. Paiva
Northern Virginia Community College

Heinle & Heinle Publishers
A Division of Wadsworth, Inc.
Boston, Massachusetts, 02116 U.S.A.

The publication of *Independent Writing* was directed by the members of the Heinle & Heinle ESL Publishing Team:

Erik Gundersen, Editorial Director
Susan Mraz, Marketing Manager
Kristin Thalheimer, Production Editor

Also participating in the publication of this program were:

Publisher: Stanley J. Galek
Editorial Production Manager: Elizabeth Holthaus
Associate Editor: Lynne Telson Barsky
Project Manager: Judy Keith
Manufacturing Coordinator: Mary Beth Lynch
Photo Coordinator: Carl Spector
Interior Designer: Christine Reynolds
Cover Illustrator: Joseph A. Osina
Cover Designer: Christi Rosso

Library of Congress Cataloging-in-Publication Data

O'Donnell, Teresa D.
    Independent Writing / Teresa D. O'Donnell, Judith L. Paiva,
        p.   cm.
    ISBN 0-8384-4206-4
    1. English language—Rhetoric. 2. English language—
Textbooks for foreign speakers.   I. Paiva, Judith L.
II. Title.
PE 1408.O33   1993
808'.042--dc20   92-40410
                                            CIP

Heinle & Heinle Publishers is a division of Wadsworth, Inc.

Manufactured in the United States of America

10 9 8 7 6 5 4 3

Dedicated to

Dr. Elaine C. Niner

in grateful appreciation for bestowing on us

wisdom, support, and love.

CONTENTS

Chapter Six
Focus on Content: Using Argumentation

PREFACE to the Second Edition

The revised second edition of *Independent Writing* continues the focus of the first edition: to help students in college-preparatory English programs at the advanced levels attain the necessary proficiency to perform academic writing at the college level. With an ordered, cumulative approach to the many facets of writing, the book helps students develop the skills they need to become competent, independent writers. It gives both students and the teacher a context in which to practice the writing process.

ESL/EFL students using this text are presumably at the 450 to 550 TOEFL range and have previously had some type of intermediate-level grammar/writing instruction. The text provides enough material for a 12- to 15-week writing course and helps students prepare for freshman-level English composition or other college-level courses upon completion.

The revisions in the second edition are based on supportive feedback from students and colleagues who used the original text and on the authors' responses to the current state of language teaching pedagogy. The second edition retains popular features of the original text, such as sample student essays and instruction in writing introductions and conclusions, while offering new, expanded activities. With additional reference to modes of rhetorical organization, it reflects an eclectic approach to writing as it balances process with product.

Features of the second edition are

- a cumulative approach to paraphrasing and **summary writing**,
- logical organization of writing and selective structure reviews,
- focus on the writing process,
- greater variety of writing opportunities, with a directed, cooperative writing and an "independent" writing in each chapter,
- cooperative learning activities in each chapter,
- updated examples, charts, and graphs,
- suggestions for computer-generated writing exercises in the chapters and in an extensive appendix.

Organization of contents

Independent Writing has an integrated organization, with writing instruction, structure review, and culminating writing assignments in each chapter. A step-by-step introduction to summary writing, so necessary for academic writing, supports the movement toward an independent writing assignment at the end of Chapter Six.

Chapter One, which introduces the writing process, begins with paragraph writing followed in Chapter Two by an introduction to the essay writing process. Students are led through the preliminary processes of limiting a topic, clarifying their purpose, writing a thesis statement, and writing an introduction. Chapter Three stresses planning and organizing, including outlining and writing a conclusion. Chapters Four and Five, which focus on suiting organization to content, introduce logical division and classification, comparison and contrast, and cause and effect. These rhetorical devices are included in the belief that most ESL/EFL students are unfamiliar with them and that they are necessary for most college English courses. These chapters also give students practice in summarizing information from charts and graphs, a skill needed in academic writing. With further focus on content, Chapter Six requires students to participate in a debate in preparation for writing an argumentative essay.

Structure reviews in each chapter focus on sentence structures necessary for coherence in writing and for the paraphrasing students will need to do in writing summaries. Sentence combining exercises at the end of Chapters One, Two, Three, and Five help students manipulate the structures they are focusing on and lead them to understand the variety of sentence structures available for expressing their ideas.

The last assignment completes the process toward independence, requiring students to use their paraphrasing and summarizing skills and materials from charts and graphs in a final, independently written essay.

Three appendices follow the last chapter. Appendix 1 is a brief review of sentence punctuation with explanations and examples of the use of the period, comma, semicolon, and quotation marks. Appendix 2 is a summary of connecting words: conjunctions, logical connectors, and adverbial expressions. Appendix 3 discusses ways in which computers can be used in the writing process and presents specific suggestions for maximizing their usefulness in both individual and collaborative writing.

Focus on the writing process

An explanation of the writing process precedes the first writing assignment in Chapter One. Specific references to following the process in the writing assignments, especially to using peer review, are made throughout the text. Appendix 3 suggests the use of computers as support for the writing process.

A variety of writing opportunities

Employing a learner-centered approach, each chapter provides a variety of writing opportunities at every stage of the writing process. In addition, each chapter (except for Chapter One) has two major writing assignments: "Writing Together" and "Writing on Your Own." In the first, content-based assignment, students work cooperatively to produce a writing. This first highly structured assignment leads students through the writing process before they write on their own.

Cooperative learning activities

Cooperative learning activities are prominent in each chapter. In Chapter Two, for example, students cooperate to produce an oral adventure story, first with the whole class and then in small groups. A small group then writes an adventure story (with each student writing a different paragraph) before narrating a story on their own. In Chapter Three, students cooperate to write directions for a picture that another group must then draw. In Chapter Six, students practice the logic of argument as they participate in a group debate before working on their own argumentative essay.

A cumulative approach to paraphrasing and summary writing

Chapters One through Five are each followed by one section of a cumulative instructional program in writing summaries. Summary writing is a skill that college students need to master. The approach in this text is based on the belief that summary writing is not easy and that students can learn it best through a step-by-step process. Thus, students are given practice in finding and restating main ideas, outlining, and paraphrasing before they are asked to write summaries. Structure review sections of the text, from a review of clause structures to paraphrasing with reported speech, support the summary-writing process. The summary writing sections are separate from each chapter so that they may be studied as a unit if desired. However, they are integral parts of the text and must be mastered in order to do the culminating exercises in Chapter Six, which require students to summarize the essays of others for use in their own argumentative essays.

In conclusion

The Second Edition of *Independent Writing* focuses on student involvement in the writing process. Like the First Edition, it assumes that the teacher will guide students through the process of prewriting, drafting, reviewing, revising, and editing. Since the aim of the text is to encourage independence in writing, it presents writing as an inherently individual process. A variety of techniques is introduced, from very structured to more self-directed activities, with the understanding that students may already have developed techniques that they are comfortable with. It is the authors' hope that by participating in the variety of writing activities in the book, students will become truly independent writers, able to proceed into their college courses with more confidence in their ability to use the English language.

To the Teacher

The Second Edition of *Independent Writing* features the use of the computer as a tool for writing. All writing assignments and summaries can be done on the computer. Following are some suggestions for using computers for specific exercises in the text (indicated by a computer symbol) and for introducing writing on the computer. Appendix 3, at the end of the book, contains additional suggestions directed to the students themselves.

Sentence Combining Exercises. Sentence combining exercises in Chapters One, Two, Three, and Five are easily done on the computer. Students can experiment with a variety of ways to combine each pair of sentences without having to recopy the sentences over and over.

1. The teacher types all five exercises on one disk as they appear in the book and makes a copy for each student.
2. The teacher uses Exercise 5 in Chapter One to introduce students to deleting and inserting text. For example: to join the sentences (1), they delete the period, *it*, and *has*, and insert *and*. To join sentences (2), they delete the period, insert *so*, and change to a small *t* on *they*.

Writing Assignments: Writing Together. Each chapter has a writing assignment done with a partner or group. The computer is an excellent medium for shared writing.

Specific suggestions are given for each assignment. For all assignments, the following seven steps should be followed once draft copy is available:

1. Copies are printed for each member of the pair or group.
2. The pair or group decides on suggestions for revision.
3. One member is chosen to type in the revisions.
4. Another member runs the spell-checker.
5. Copies are printed again.
6. Each member edits the copy.
7. Another member types in the editing suggestions and prints the final copy.

■ **Chapter One:** *Writing a Paragraph Together.* The first writing assignment is used to introduce students to collaborative writing. Students compose a paragraph together, with the better typist at the keyboard, and both students make suggestions for the content. Because both students can see the screen easily, collaboration is much more effective. After the paragraph is finished, two copies are printed. (Continue with suggestions 1-7 preceding.)

■ **Chapter Two:** *Writing an Adventure Story Together.* In order to write the story on the computer, students need to be given time to work on the story over a period of days. Each group of writers is to have one disk. The first writer enters the beginning. Each successive writer accesses what is on the disk and adds another paragraph, following the directions for the assignment, until the story is finished. Copies are printed for each member of the group. (Continue with suggestions 1-7 preceding.)

■ **Chapter Three:** *Writing Directions Together.* Each group of students has one disk. After students have brainstormed ideas, an outline is produced on the computer with all students sitting around the screen. Once the outline is completed, students divide the tasks of writing, with one assigned the introduction, one or more the middle, and another (perhaps the same person that wrote the introduction) the conclusion.

Over a period of days, students enter the part of the text they were assigned, starting with the introduction, the body, and then the conclusion. Copies are printed. (Continue with suggestions 1-7 preceding.)

■ **Chapter Four:** *Writing a Comparison Together.* Each group of students has one disk. Students discuss each graph or chart and draw conclusions, which are typed in by the student at the keyboard. Copies of the conclusions are printed for each member of the group.

One member of the group types the outline as the group discusses and decides on an organizational pattern for the essay. A copy of the outline is printed for each member. A part of the essay is assigned to each member. Following the outline, each student writes one paragraph of the body, using information from the charts and graphs. After all body paragraphs are entered on one disk, students collaborate to write the introduction and conclusion and add any necessary cohesive devices. Copies are printed. (Continue with suggestions 1-7 preceding.)

■ **Chapter Five:** *Writing About Causes and Effects Together.* Each group of students has one disk. After the students have read the articles and listed the causes and effects, they work together to decide on their focus and on a thesis statement. Variations of thesis statements are entered in a file on the computer; the group members select the one they like the best.

Next, the students develop an outline. Many word-processing programs have outline formats that may be used. Each student takes a print-out of the outline.

The final stage is to divide the task of writing the first draft. Students can take turns entering their part of the text onto the disk during the next class period or between class if the computers are available for out-of-class use. (Continue with suggestions 1-7 preceding.)

■ **Chapter Six:** *Writing an Argument Together.* As the research on the names mentioned in the George Will article is completed, each group member enters the information on a file named RESEARCH. Information is entered in alphabetical order by the last name of the person studied. Each student receives a print-out of the research file to refer to in discussing the proposal to change U.S. currency and in developing supporting statements or counter-arguments.

In another file, the group works together to list the reasons why they agree or disagree with the proposal. From this list, an outline may be developed using the outline format on the word-processing program. Each student receives a print-out of the list and the outline.

Group members will each need a disk for this part of the assignment. Each group member now drafts his or her own reaction to the article. The group members may want to work together on the summary part of the essay, but they will develop their own opinions in writing personal reactions to the proposal. If the group writes the summary jointly, each will receive a print-out of the summary.

After writing the draft, each student follows these steps:

1. Decide on revisions. The student may share a print-out of his or her draft with a partner to get feedback.

2. Type the revisions.

3. Run the spell-checker.

4. Edit the copy for grammar and punctuation. (Again, partners may work together on this step.)

5. Print the final copy.

ACKNOWLEDGMENTS

Producing a textbook is by nature a collaborative effort, and the authors gratefully acknowledge the support of all who have, directly or indirectly, contributed to this project. To Dr. Richard J. Ernst, President, Northern Virginia Community College, goes our gratitude for his encouragement of our work and his permission to use the photos of our college found in this text. We thank all of our wonderful friends, students, and colleagues, some of whom are present in essays or photographs throughout these pages, who have given us food for thought and useful advice as they tested some of the teaching strategies we have employed here. A special bouquet to Nancy Lorentz, who cheerfully dealt with computer glitches and printer problems in aiding us with the production of the manuscript. We especially wish to thank our editor at Heinle & Heinle, Erik Gunderson, his associate, Lynne Telson Barsky, our production editor, Kristin Thalheimer, our project manager, Judy Keith, and Talbot F. Hamlin for their invaluable advice and expertise. Finally, a loving thanks to our families, especially our children, Rachel, Juan, and Shana, who have believed in us and given us continued encouragement throughout this project.

Teresa D. O'Donnell
Judith L. Paiva

Chapter One
Writing Paragraphs

PARAGRAPH WRITING

Most writing is made up of smaller units called *paragraphs,* identified by visual representation and by contents. The first line of a paragraph, especially if handwritten, is indented (begun a few spaces to the right of the margin) to indicate the beginning of the paragraph.

A paragraph can also be identified by its contents, a group of related sentences that support the writer's main idea. Here is an example.

> <u>Automobiles are expensive and often inconvenient necessities in modern life</u>. It is true that living without a car is almost impossible in many American cities because public transportation is often expensive and not very accessible, and distances between businesses and residential areas are too great for people to commute by bicycle or by walking. However, there are also disadvantages to automobile ownership. In the first place, people pay a lot of money, often including high sales tax, to buy an automobile; insurance, licenses, gas, oil, and maintenance fees are also expensive. After all of these bills are paid, drivers often have trouble finding parking spots. Once they do, they pay high parking fees at downtown lots near their offices. Worst of all, if the "dream machines" break down, as they inevitably do, the drivers not only have to pay high repair bills, but they are once more without transportation while the cars are in the repair shop. Maybe life was easier when a person could hop outside the front door onto a friendly horse and trot down to Main Street!

What are the essentials of a paragraph?

Topic sentences: A paragraph has a main idea expressed in a topic sentence. This sentence may appear at the beginning, in the middle, or at the end of a paragraph. In the preceding paragraph, the main idea is "Automobiles are expensive and often inconvenient necessities in modern life." This main idea sentence (also called the topic sentence) serves several purposes:

1. It introduces the main idea of the paragraph. In this case, *"Automobiles are expensive and often inconvenient necessities in modern life."*

2. It limits the topic of the paragraph. In this example, the topic is limited to the expenses and inconveniences of owning a car, not the pleasures or dangers or some other aspect of owning a car. The word *expensive* controls the idea and indicates the focus of the topic.

3. It often suggests how the paragraph will be developed. From the topic sentence of the example paragraph, we assume that the paragraph will discuss both the expenses and inconveniences of driving a car.

Supporting sentences: A paragraph has main supporting ideas, all relating to the topic sentence. The writer of the sample paragraph on page 2 chose the following supporting ideas:

1. Most people need cars in the United States.
2. They have to pay a lot of money to buy a car.
3. They have to pay for licenses.
4. They have to pay for insurance.
5. They have to buy gas and oil.
6. They have to pay for maintenance.
7. Drivers have trouble finding parking places.
8. They have to pay parking fees.
9. Cars break down.

Details: The supporting ideas may themselves be further supported by facts, details, or statistics. In a longer paragraph, under the first supporting sentence, we might add statistics telling how many cars are owned by people in the United States and how many families own two or more automobiles.

Logical order: The ideas in the paragraph must be presented in logical order. In the sample paragraph, the ideas are presented in the order of time. When we buy a car, our first expense is the cost of the car itself; next, we pay for local and state licenses; then comes auto insurance, and so forth. It wouldn't be logical to write first about paying for insurance because buying the car is the first step in the process. Chronological, or time, order is especially important in a paragraph showing a process (how something is done), but all ideas are presented in some logical order.

Logical connectors: To indicate this progression of ideas and to provide an orderly connection between the ideas (coherence), writers use logical connecting words, also called "transition" words. These words not only help the flow of ideas, but also indicate the relationship between ideas (chronological, causal, etc.). In the following example, the logical connectors (underlined) indicate the steps in the process of buying a car:

> Buying a car requires special planning. <u>First</u>, we need to arrange for the money to pay for the car. We may take out a bank loan, borrow from our parents, or save money from our salaries. <u>Next</u>, we must find a car that suits our pocketbook and our needs. <u>After making our purchase</u>, we must then arrange for auto insurance. <u>In addition</u>, we must buy a license plate and pay for the car inspection.

Concluding sentence: A paragraph may have a concluding sentence. In the case of the first sample paragraph about the expenses of owning a car, the final sentence restates the main idea in a different way.

> Maybe life was easier when a person could hop outside the front door onto a friendly horse and trot down to Main Street!

This is an indirect and amusing way of saying that owning a car is an inconvenient necessity in modern life.

Unity and coherence: When a paragraph includes a sequence of sentences that are all related to the topic sentence, it is *unified*. A paragraph that has a continuous line of thought that passes from sentence to sentence is *coherent.* The introductory paragraph about buying a car has unity because all of the sentences relate to the topic sentence. Transitional words, such as *however* and *after all,* and pronoun references, such as *these bills* and *they,* give the paragraph coherence. An effective paragraph is both unified and coherent.

Exercise 1. Identifying Parts of Common Types of Paragraphs

The kinds of supporting materials used in paragraphs depend on the topic sentence and the purpose of the paragraph as part of a whole written composition. The following paragraphs exemplify common types.

As you look at each paragraph, think about the main idea or topic sentence. Does it have a word or phrase that controls the idea of the paragraph? What are the main supporting ideas? Are there any logical connectors? Is there a conclusion?

1. A paragraph with *examples* (single items that serve as models or samples):

   My friend Nhuong is a very hard-working man. Although he has to work in a soft drink plant for eight hours each day, he also attends English classes at a community center. After his daily classes, he hurries to the plant, where he works until 1:00 a.m., standing in the assembly line inspecting bottles. He has to do most of his studying on weekends and also try to find some time to be with his family and friends. His relatives, who have just immigrated to the United States, live with him, and he must help them adjust to American life. Nhuong doesn't have much time to sleep or relax, but he never complains. In fact, he seems to enjoy working so much that some people think he's a "workaholic."

   Topic/main idea _____

   Controlling phrase or word _____

Supporting ideas

1. _____

2. _____

3. _____

4. _____

Logical connectors _____

Conclusion _____

2. A paragraph with an *illustration* (material that presents clarification or explanation to prove a point):

    Not knowing a language well can sometimes cause a problem in communicating. One word in a language can have different meanings, or two words can have the same pronunciation but have different meanings. About two years ago, one of my friends told me an embarrassing story. The first year she was in the United States, she had a job at a dry-cleaning establishment. One day a customer came in to pick up his clothes. After he had paid for the cleaning and was ready to leave, he suddenly turned back to my friend and asked, "Do you dye here?" Thinking that she had understood his question, my friend got upset and answered, "No, I won't die here. I want to die in my own country!"

Topic/main idea _____

Controlling phrase or word _____

Supporting ideas

1. _____

2. _____

Logical connectors _____

Conclusion _____

3. A paragraph with *facts* (figures and statistics that can be proven or verified):

    Mount Everest was first surveyed in 1852, when it was found to be the highest mountain in the world. First, it was measured to be 29,000 feet. Later, however, someone added two feet so the height would not appear to be a round number estimate. In 1954, another team surveyed and reported the mountain to be 29,028 feet. No matter which figure is used, there is no doubt that no other mountain peak in the world is as high as Mount Everest.

Topic/main idea _____

Controlling phrase or word _____

Supporting ideas

1. _____

2. _____

Logical connectors _____

Conclusion _____

4. A paragraph with *description:*

I'll never forget the first time I saw a traditional Christmas tree. As a small child, I thought that it was the most beautiful thing that I had ever seen. I was first attracted by the bright red and green lights that seemed to sparkle all over. Then, as I drew closer to the tree, my eyes focused on what looked like miniature wooden toys hanging from colored strings and ribbons. Next to those tiny miniatures were glass balls of many different colors reflecting the lights of the tree; some of them were also painted with pictures of people dancing in the snow or skating on ponds. At the tip of each branch, someone had carefully hung a tiny candy cane, a treat to dazzle any small child, and under the tree was a tiny village with lighted houses and a sleigh pulled by reindeer and Santa Claus sitting in it. Most memorable of all, at the top of the tree was the most beautiful sight for my small eyes: a golden angel with silver threads in her white, flowing hair.

Topic/main idea _____

Controlling phrase or word _____

Supporting ideas

1. _____

2. _____

3. _____

4. _____

5. _____

6. _____

Logical connectors _____

Conclusion _____

5. A paragraph with *enumeration* (a list of ideas named one by one):

According to the 1991 World Almanac, a huge growth in urban areas in the world is taking place. It is estimated that by the year 2000 there will be forty-two metropolitan areas in the world with a population of over five million people each while in 1990 there were only thirty-four such cities. With urban populations growing so rapidly, controlled growth will be impossible, and the consequences of this situation will be very negative. For one thing, there will be sprawling slums, since there won't be enough low-cost housing available. In addition, there will be massive, regular failures of electric power and water services because of the excessive demands. Moreover, the cost of these services will sky-rocket, again as a result of the supply not being able to keep up with the demand. For another thing, there will be extensive unemployment and strained educational and recreational facilities. Roads and highways, already at capacity in many urban areas, will become even more overcrowded, resulting in enormous traffic jams. Looking forward to these things, perhaps we should all return to the quiet life of the rural countryside.

Topic/main idea _____

Controlling phrase or word _____

Supporting ideas

1. _____

2. _____

3. _____

4. _____

5. _____

Logical connectors _____

Conclusion _____

Exercise 2. Using Logical Connectors

In the exercises that follow, a topic sentence, supporting ideas, and logical connectors are listed. Use these phrases to write sentences, and join the sentences using the indicated logical connectors to write a complete, smooth-flowing paragraph.

1. *Topic sentence:*

   Life in a refugee camp is not easy.

   Supporting ideas:

   not enough food to eat

   scarce water for drinking or washing

   limited space

   no utilities (electricity, running water)

   Logical connectors:

   for one thing

   for another thing

   also

   furthermore

2. *Topic sentence:*

A community college and a university differ in several ways.

Supporting ideas:

community college: two years

university: four years

community college: A.A. degree

university: B.A. or B.S. degree; graduate degrees

community college: students come from the immediate surrounding community

university: students come from all over the state, the country, and different nations

community college: "commuter campus"

university: dormitories for students

Logical connectors:

one difference is

a second distinction is

still another is

finally

3. *Topic sentence:*

We learn to speak and write a second language in three important ways.

Supporting ideas:

follow a model (a native speaker)

receive formal instruction

practice constantly

Logical connectors:

one way is

in addition

the most important way is

Exercise 3. Identifying Irrelevant or Off-Topic Sentences

Each sentence in a paragraph supports the topic. Unrelated sentences may distract or confuse the reader. The underlined sentences in the following paragraph don't relate directly to the topic.

One of the recent status symbols for American business people is the personal beeper. These beepers may be carried in people's briefcases or hooked to their belts. <u>Fax machines have also become symbols of success</u>

for many white-collar workers. With the beepers, a person can receive messages at any time and any place. Many people also have cellular phones in their cars so that they can make calls while traveling. Nowadays, people who own beepers will never miss an important phone call; on the other hand, they can never avoid receiving unwanted messages, either. Regardless of possible disadvantages, this recent innovation in the communications field is still selling at record rates.

In the following paragraphs, draw a line through any off-topic sentence. Sometimes off-topic sentences seem to be related, but closer analysis reveals that they are related to other supporting sentences rather than directly to the topic sentence.

1. Life is a little war every day. When I mention "war," I am not talking about a conflict between two nations; I am talking about our own everyday existence. Sometimes our days are simply wonderful. From the time we get up in the morning to the time we go back to bed, we have to face many problems. I usually go to bed at 11:00 every night. For example, you get home at 6:30 p.m.; you are tired and hungry, but you have to make dinner. Food prices are skyrocketing these days. The baby starts crying and you start to get nervous about all of this. They say that being nervous can cause heart attacks. My cousin, who is a doctor, says that many people have heart disease. Then your spouse has an evening meeting, so you are left alone with a fussy baby. You would really rather sit quietly and read the newspaper, but you know it is your duty to amuse your child. This is the moment when you have to face that little war to fight your nervous system and control yourself.

2. The pronunciation of a word in a new language can sometimes be difficult and cause problems. When I was in high school, our school was very large, and there was a large foreign student population. I had a friend who had problems with pronunciation. Once, she was with me on a bus, and the bus was about to pass her stop. In trying to reach the bell, she accidentally stepped on the feet of an elderly gentleman sitting in front of her. Trying to apologize, she said what sounded like, "Kiss me, please." Public transportation usually provides priority seating for the elderly or the handicapped. The poor gentleman looked so startled that he got up and left the bus at the wrong stop. I was laughing so hard that my friend became angry. Finally, I was able to explain to her that the correct pronunciation was, "Excuse me."

3. You discover the meaning of true friendship when you are in trouble. One day, I locked my car door before taking the key out of the ignition. After I came back to the car, I knew I was in trouble. I tried to get in touch with a friend by phone, but I couldn't. Also, I was unable to find a policeman to help me. Policemen don't get enough credit for all the dangerous work they have to do. Finally, I asked a passerby for help. He

immediately took off his coat and tried hard to open a window. It was a rather warm day for March. In fact, the whole winter had been very mild. Using a piece of metal he found on the street, he was able to pry open a small space near the lock and open my car door. I was so relieved that I forgot to ask his name and phone number, but I always think of him as a good friend even though I had never seen him before in my life. I didn't have my address book with me anyway.

STRUCTURE REVIEW: Coordination

Two complete sentences (often called independent clauses) that express related ideas may be joined to make one coherent sentence. Consider the following two ideas:

It has been raining for two days. (independent clause)

The school picnic has been canceled. (independent clause)

Although the reader may understand the relationship between the two sentences without any connecting word between them, the writer can make that relationship clearer by using some type of connecting word.

It has been raining for two days, so the school picnic has been canceled.

It has been raining for two days; therefore, the school picnic has been canceled.

By using connecting words, the writer has made the cause/effect relationship between the sentences clearer. The table that follows lists the three types of words used to connect independent clauses. For each *conjunction* (column 1) you can see that there is a *logical connector* (column 2) with corresponding meaning. Listed in column 3 are *correlatives* (paired conjunctions).

Table 1. Coordination

	1. Conjunctions	*2. Logical Connectors*	*3. Correlatives*
Addition	and	also in addition besides moreover	not only... but also
Contrast/ concession	but yet	however nevertheless on the other hand still	—
Choice or alternative	or nor	otherwise	either...or neither...nor
Result	so	therefore thus as a result accordingly for this reason consequently	—
Restatement	—	in short in other words in effect	—
Restatement to intensify	—	in fact as a matter of fact indeed	—
Cause	for*	—	—

*"For" operates like the adverbial conjunction "because," but it is usually considered a conjunction.

What are some of the differences between these types of sentence connectors?

Punctuation: Even though conjunctions and logical connectors have similar meanings, the punctuation for them is different. Conjunctions are preceded by a comma (,). Logical connectors are preceded by a semicolon (;) or a period (.) and followed by a comma, as the following sentences show. (Also see Appendix 2.)

We ran to the bus stop, but the bus had already left.
> We ran to the bus stop; however, the bus had already left.

You need to study hard, or you won't pass the test.
> You need to study hard. Otherwise, you won't pass the test.

Position: Conjunctions always come between two independent clauses. Some logical connectors may come in two other positions as in these sentences (notice how they are punctuated):

> I've visited many countries in the world. I've never been to India, however.

> I've visited many countries in the world. I've never, however, been to India.

Using neither, nor, never: When the conjunction *nor* connects two sentences, the word order in the second sentence changes to question word order rather than statement word order. This same rule applies whenever a negative word, such as *neither* or *never*, precedes a clause.

> I haven't done the research paper yet, <u>nor have I</u> finished the required lab work.

> John doesn't speak Spanish, <u>nor do</u> his parents.

Using paired conjunctions: Changes in word order are required with some of the correlative (paired) conjunctions from column 3 when they are used to join sentences.

> <u>Either</u> you will have to quiet down, <u>or</u> you will be asked to leave the lecture.

> <u>Neither</u> did he finish his research paper, <u>nor</u> did he take the final exam.

> <u>Not only</u> is this the last time I'll help you, <u>but</u> it is <u>also</u> the last time I'll remind you to do this work.

Note: The change in word order is not necessary when joining parts of sentences:

> Sally, my athletic sister, was good at <u>not only</u> tennis <u>but also</u> golf.

Exercise 1. Selecting Conjunctions

Combine the following sentences, using appropriate conjunctions from Table 1. Be sure that your choice of conjunctions illustrates the relationship between the paired sentences and that you punctuate correctly. The first has been done for you.

1. I would like to go to the meeting.
   I have to work tonight.
   I would like to go to the meeting, but I have to work tonight.

2. Taking the bus is cheaper than driving.
   It conserves energy.

   _____

   _____

3. The skier broke his leg.
   He couldn't compete in the Olympics.

   _____

   _____

4. Students may not smoke in class.
   They may not eat in class. (use _nor_)

   _____

   _____

5. Zoo animals must not be fed by visitors.
   Some snack foods are harmful to their health.

   _____

   _____

6. The family next door had just moved in.
   The neighbors had a welcoming party for them.

   _____

   _____

7. Butter is very expensive.
   Most people buy margarine.

   _____

   _____

8. I bought a large car two years ago.
   Now I wish I had bought a small one.

   _____

   _____

9. Robert is a lazy student.
   He misses a lot of classes.

   _____

   _____

10. Would you like to go to a movie?
    Would you rather go ice skating?

    _____

    _____

Exercise 2. Selecting Logical Connectors

Use appropriate connectors to link the ideas in the following sentences. Try to put the sentence connectors in different positions, and be sure to punctuate correctly! The first one has been done for you.

1. The old woman had seventeen children.
   She owned twelve cats!

   The old woman had seventeen children. In addition, she owned twelve cats!

2. Working part time gives you more free time.
   You don't earn as much money as full-time workers do.

   _____

   _____

3. This school will be closed next year.
   The children will be bussed to another school.

   _____

   _____

4. The president of that country is repressive and cruel.
   He is a tyrant.

   _____

   _____

5. I'm sure you are a very intelligent person.
   You can't type, so I can't hire you.

   _____

   _____

6. This type of flour is not made in the United States.
   I can't make the Oriental cake I told you about.

   _____

   _____

7. People should exercise regularly.
   They will get out of shape.

   _____

   _____

8. Barbara is quite a bit taller than most women.
   She is six inches taller than her husband.

   _____

   _____

9. Keep your dog quiet.
   I will call the police.

   _____

   _____

10. I would like to take an English literature course.
    I haven't had the prerequisites yet.

    _____

    _____

Exercise 3. Inserting Correlative Conjunctions

Combine the following sentences, using the given correlatives. Remember to combine sentences, not parts of sentences, and to reverse the subject-verb word order where necessary. The first has been done for you.

1. The voters are angry.
   They feel shocked at his attitude. (not only..., but also)
   Not only are the voters angry, but they also feel shocked at his attitude.

2. Say something constructive.
   Don't say anything at all. (either..., or)

   _____

   _____

3. Americans pay income tax.
   They are charged high sales taxes in some states. (not only..., but also)

   _____

   _____

4. He didn't ask my permission.
   He didn't give me an explanation of his action. (neither..., nor)
   (Remember to use affirmative verbs.)

   _____

   _____

5. Mr. Parker will move to France.
   He will change jobs and stay here. (either..., or)

   _____

   _____

6. In planning for their careers, people must consider their own special interests.

   They must take the job market into careful consideration. (not only..., but also)

   _____

   _____

7. She decided to change her major.
   She decided to change universities. (not only..., but also)

   _____

   _____

8. The architect didn't design the building to be modern.
   She didn't design it to be attractive. (neither..., nor)

   _____

   _____

9. John has read all of the books in the library on the world's great religions.

   He has read as much as he can about religious cults. (not only..., but also)

   _____

   _____

10. The psychology department didn't offer any courses in abnormal behavior last semester.
    It didn't offer any courses in human relations. (neither..., nor)

    _____

    _____

Exercise 4. Using Conjunctions, Correlatives, and Logical Connectors

Fill in the blanks with appropriate conjunctions, correlatives, or logical connectors. The punctuation will give you clues as to which connecting type to use. Refer to Table 1 on p. 11 for a variety of choices.

Working in a large U.S. city can be exciting; _____ , it can also cause problems. The noise from traffic can be irritating, _____ the fumes from automobiles are dangerous. People often spend hours in traffic every day, so they inhale dangerous gases such as carbon monoxide. Of course, not everyone drives to work in a city. Either people can accept the inconveniences of waiting for public transportation, _____ they can try to get a taxi. _____ , taxis tend to disappear when it is raining. They are convenient when available, _____ they are an expensive means of transportation. _____ is transportation in a large city expensive and time-consuming, _____ it can _____ be dangerous. Muggings occur frequently on city streets, _____ crimes are often committed on subways. _____ , going to work in a large city is frequently irritating, dangerous, and expensive.

Exercise 5. Sentence Combining

The more developed writer in English uses sentences that are connected to show the relationships between them. Use what you have learned about coordinating structures to do this exercise.

On a piece of paper, rewrite the paragraph. Use coordinating structures to combine the sentences with the same numbers into one sentence. Unnumbered sentences should be included but not combined with others. When you finish, you should have a nicely developed, cohesive paragraph. If you will be using a computer in your writing, this would be a good time to read Appendix 3, "Computers and the Writing Process," (page 209).

(1) A coin is a piece of metal that has a certain weight. *(1)* It has the mark of the people who issued it. *(2)* The Lydians were a powerful people in Asia Minor who needed a convenient method of receiving payment for products they produced. *(2)* They made the first coins in the seventh century B.C. These primitively made coins were composed of "electrum," a natural composition of gold and silver. *(3)* The Greeks saw these coins and appreciated their usefulness. *(3)* They began to make coins, too. *(4)* About 100 years later, many cities in Greece had coins. *(4)* Cities all over the mainland of Asia Minor had them, too. *(5)* Gold coins were the most valuable. *(5)* Silver and copper were also used. The Romans later adopted the idea, carrying it on for 500 years, when the art of coinage declined. *(6)* In the fifteenth century, the art of coinage was revived because there was more metal available. *(6)* There were many skilled artists to engrave the coins in this period of history. *(7)* The first coins made in America, in 1752, were

not regular in shape. *(7)* They were not the same weight. *(8)* Today, coins are essential in our modern life. *(8)* Our society, with its vast numbers of coin-operated machines, could not function without this ancient invention.

INTRODUCTION TO THE WRITING PROCESS

Few writers are able to write exactly what they want to say and how they want to say it the first time they sit down to write. In fact, other than writing personal letters to family and friends, most writers make many changes before they finish writing. People who write for business, authors of books and novels, lawyers, and anyone who has to produce writing of any kind all know that writing involves a number of steps before they achieve a finished product.

This writing process involves a series of tasks: thinking, planning, writing (rewriting), and editing. Writers go through this process in different ways. Some begin with thinking and planning before writing. Others start right out writing. Each writer has a preferred way of working through the process.

Look at the writing process as a large circle with four quadrants, each one part of the process.

Moving around the circle, we pass through the various steps. The circle has no end, however, and as we continue around the circle, we keep passing through the steps. We begin to understand that writing is a *recursive* activity. This means that we may not go through the steps only once. We often return to steps that we have gone through before.

Thinking   How does this work? Let's start with *thinking.* At the thinking stage, we use a variety of strategies for getting ideas. We might talk about a subject with our friends and classmates individually or in a group. This talking (or brainstorming) will help us generate more of our own ideas. We might take a blank piece of paper and randomly list ideas that come to us as we think about the topic. We might put our ideas on note cards, or we might even just keep them quietly in our heads.

Planning   Once we have our ideas, we may move on to the *planning* stage before beginning to write. Some of us may like to make a written sketch or outline of our ideas. We can put our ideas in order and arrange and rearrange them during this step. Then we have a plan to follow before beginning to write.

Writing   Others of us may prefer to skip the planning step at this point and move directly to *writing.* Once we have ideas, we are ready to put them all down on paper before any planning. Then we look at what we have written, evaluate how we have presented our ideas, and then make a plan for reordering them before writing again.

As a matter of fact, for many writers, the first step is writing, not thinking or planning. They use writing about ideas to help them generate new ideas. Their thinking takes place while they write. Planning comes later.

Revising   Part of the writing stage is *revising,* looking at the content of what we have written and asking several questions: Have I put my ideas down in an order that will be logical to the reader? Have I explained my ideas in enough detail to make them clear? Have I used connecting words and sentences to make my writing coherent?

We may think that our writing is logical, clear, and coherent. However, our peers are usually able to read our writing more critically. Just as professional writers use editors to help revise their writing, we can use our classmates to give us useful feedback. These *peer editors* are a helpful part of the writing process.

Editing   What about final editing? Although we often think of editing (finding errors in spelling, punctuation, sentence sense, etc.) as the last step in the process, it is likely to go on all the time we are writing. Just as with revising, it is useful to have the help of a peer editor at this stage, but we must also learn to do *self-editing* before handing in our final drafts to the teacher.

Writing is a spiraling process that takes us through a series of activities. As we look again at the circle, we see that we may start with writing or thinking. We may plan before or while writing. We may move around the circle many times going back and forth through the steps, even changing our principal idea or thesis, until we write a final copy.

This process should be used as you do the writing activities in this text. In most writing assignments, suggestions are given to involve you and your classmates in the process as you learn to write together.

WRITING ASSIGNMENT:

Writing a Paragraph Together

This first writing assignment requires that you write a paragraph with a classmate. Choose one of the topics (A, B, C, or D) and follow this writing process to produce your final draft together:

1. Brainstorm (talk together) for ideas. Jot down your ideas.

2. Discuss how you will order your ideas.

3. Write a first draft together.

4. Read over the draft to check for clarity of ideas and to make sure that you have the essential parts of a paragraph: a topic sentence with a controlling idea; main supporting ideas; enough details; logical connectors; a conclusion.

5. Write a second draft and repeat the review process together.

6. Edit your draft together for errors in spelling, punctuation, grammar, or sentence structure. Try to use structures of coordination where appropriate.

TOPICS

A. Description

With your partner, write a description of a person, object, or place you are both familiar with. Before you begin writing, visualize your topic and discuss with your classmate what you think should be included in the description. Take some notes. Then write a descriptive paragraph with your partner.

B. Enumerating Ideas

With your partner, decide on three or four of the most important decisions that a person must be prepared to make in life. In preparation, think about some of the important choices that you have had to make. As you plan your paragraph, think about the order of your ideas. You might want to list them in order of importance. Write a paragraph with your partner.

C. Facts or Statistics

(This topic is especially useful if you and your partner do not know each other very well.) You and your partner are to interview each other. Ask each other about background, home country, jobs, experiences, etc. Try to find out one or two unusual facts about each other. Then write a paragraph in which you relate some of the facts that you have learned about your partner. Exchange papers and read what your partner wrote about you. Is all the information correct? Work with your partner to produce final drafts of your papers.

D. Examples

With your partner, define the ideal doctor, teacher, or other professional person. Think about someone you know or have personal knowledge about who exemplifies the qualities you believe this professional should possess. Make a list of the personal or physical qualities this ideal person should have. Write a paragraph with your partner that combines your ideas.

SUMMARY WRITING
Part One: Introduction to Summary Writing

Being able to summarize skillfully is a useful tool. It can help you to study and to complete many of your writing assignments. You are often required to do large amounts of reading for college courses. Finding main ideas in what you read and writing these ideas down succinctly makes your studying more efficient. Also, you are asked to produce different kinds of writing in college classes. Sometimes teachers will ask you to make reports on outside readings or to include the ideas of other authors in your research papers. In each case, you must know how to summarize.

What is a summary?

- It is a shortened version of another author's writing.
- It includes only the most important information.
- It can be any length depending on the amount of information from the original text that is included.
- It is written *in your own words*.
- It includes only the ideas from the original text, not your response to those ideas.

What do you need to do before you write a summary?

- You need to read the text several times and possibly discuss it with someone else.
- You need to understand the original text thoroughly.
- You need to identify the main ideas in the text.

The following exercises and others in this text will help you begin to learn the process of writing summaries.

Exercise 1. Finding Main Ideas

In the following paragraphs, identify the topic and underline the main idea sentence. The main idea sentence is *not* always the first sentence in the paragraph. Also, underline any logical connectors and the concluding sentence if there is one.

1. Each step in a Japanese tea ceremony is important. First, guests kneel on a woven straw mat on the floor. The tea master may serve sweet cakes. Then, he or she will begin the careful preparation of the tea. A special

powdered tea, either thick tea or thin tea, is measured into a bowl. Water heated to exactly the right temperature is then poured in. The tea master must know exactly when the tea is ready to be served. When ready, it is poured into individual bowls and handed to each guest. The temperature must be not too hot and not too cold. The good taste of the tea is important, but the simplicity and delicate beauty of the service are equally respected.

2. Although bamboo bends like grass, it can be as strong as steel. Some kinds grow so fast that if you are patient, you can see them grow about two inches per hour. No other plant has so many uses for animals and people. For example, it is used as a food by animals such as Pandas, as medicine by people in many cultures, and as a symbol in many religious and cultural ceremonies. Because of its strength and flexibility, it is used in the construction of houses and even large buildings to reinforce concrete and to make scaffolds. Bamboo is truly a "magic" plant.

3. Though most countries today are no longer governed by monarchs, kings and queens and other members of royal families in some countries still have important roles to play. The royal family of England is just one example. This royal family, headed presently by Queen Elizabeth II, though politically powerless, still serves as a strong symbolic force. The wedding of Prince Charles and Princess Diana was an example of the interest people still have in royalty. Beatrix, Queen of the Netherlands and Margrethe of Denmark are other examples. Both consider their roles important. Beatrix, as a working mother, divides her time between serving her country and taking care of her children. Margrethe is a representative of her country to other nations. Many members of royalty, such as the journalist Prince Tomahito of Japan, have jobs and spend their lives much as ordinary citizens do, but they still play important roles as symbolic heads of their countries.

4. The type of armor worn by soldiers, fighters, and knights evolved gradually in Europe during the Middle Ages. First, it consisted of specially treated leather worn on the legs, chest, and arms. It offered slight protection but didn't protect the body from heavy blows. Later, leather was combined with *chain mail,* a type of armor made of small loops of iron or steel. It was almost as flexible as cloth or leather, but it was very heavy. As time went on, other types of metal armor were used. Armor made of metal plates fitted the shape of the body and had metal joints which let the arms and legs move. However, it weighed as much as 100 pounds. Men in such armor had to be lifted onto their horses with a crane, and if they were knocked off their horses in battle, they couldn't move. As armor became more protective, it became more expensive, heavy, and

slow. With the development of firearms, it was somewhat abandoned, until recently when police officers have begun to wear armor in the form of bulletproof vests.

5.   The Chinese language developed without an alphabet to represent sounds, so each Chinese word, or character, has a different form. Students have to learn thousands of characters to read and write Chinese well. This difficulty of writing Chinese has had a profound effect on China's history. In the past, only the rich could afford time to learn to read and write. Since all government officials had to be able to read and write, farmers and laborers rarely qualified for these jobs. Consequently, it was mainly the wealthy who ran the government.

In summary writing, you first have to identify the author's main idea, as you did in Exercise 1 on page 22. However, you cannot copy the main idea sentence (if there is one) directly into your summary because the summary must be written *in your own words*. The next exercise gives you practice choosing *restated* main ideas.

Exercise 2. Restating Main Ideas

Read each paragraph and underline the main idea sentence. Then, choose the sentence that best *restates* that main idea.

1.   In 1940, William H. Sheldon devised a system of classifying human body types that is still used today. His classification was based on the 3 layers of cells in the developing embryo: the inner layer, which develops into the digestive organs; the middle layer, which develops into the skeleton; the outer layer, which develops into the skin, hair, nails, and nervous system. According to his theory, these layers develop differently in each person. In different people, different layers predominate. The body types are: 1) Endomorph. This type has a soft body with bulges in places and strong muscles which may be hidden in fat; 2) Mesomorph. This type has well-developed muscles all over, with large bones and a great need for physical activity; 3) Ectomorph. This type is very active, thin, and lean, with small bones, thin chest, prominent ribs, a flat stomach, and long, thin arms and legs. Most people are a combination of types.

_____ a. William Sheldon devised a system of classifying human body types in 1940.

_____ b. Based on the layers of cells of the developing embryo, Sheldon's system of classification is still used to identify human body types.

_____ c. The three human body types are: endomorph, mesomorph, and ectomorph.

2. Most cultures have superstitious beliefs. Many share the belief that breaking a mirror will bring seven years of bad luck or cause the death of someone in the family. What is the origin of this superstition? Before mirrors were invented, people gazed at their reflections in pools, ponds, and lakes. A distorted image meant impending disaster. Early Greeks and Egyptians valued "unbreakable" metal mirrors as magical. When glass mirrors were introduced, the Romans marked a broken mirror as bad luck. The seven year length of the misfortune came from the Roman belief that a person's body rejuvenated every seven years, when he or she became, in effect, a new person.

_____ a. The shared belief that a broken mirror will bring bad luck originated with the Romans.

_____ b. Many cultures have superstitious beliefs.

_____ c. Greeks and Egyptians valued metal mirrors for their magical properties.

3. The meaning of a spoken sentence depends partly upon which word or words we emphasize. In the sentence, "You dropped the glass," different meaning is conveyed by stressing different words: "You dropped the *glass*" (not the cup) or "*You* dropped the glass" (not Mary or Jim). One sentence can be said in a variety of ways, emphasizing different words, resulting in vastly different meanings.

_____ a. Sentences have different meanings.

_____ b. Stress is important in sentences.

_____ c. Words in sentences have accents.

4. Astrologists have always claimed to be able to tell someone's personality from knowledge of planetary positions. Now, however, scientists at the University of California have shown that astrologists cannot make that claim. Personality profiles of three subjects plus a natal chart (a chart containing information about the position of the planets at the time of one's birth) for one of them were sent to each of two dozen astrologists. They were asked to choose the personality profile that best matched the natal chart. The astrologists were able to pick the personality profile in just one out of three of the cases, a rate that is no better than chance. Scientists concluded that astrology had flunked the test.

_____ a. Astrologists at the University of California know about planets.

_____ b. Scientists have proved that astrologists make false claims.

_____ c. A natal chart is about a person's personality.

Chapter Two
Beginning the Essay Process

WHAT IS AN ESSAY?

The first chapter reviewed the structure of an individual paragraph: the topic sentence with the key word or controlling idea, the supporting sentences, the transitions, and the conclusion. From now on in this text, we will look at the paragraph as a part of a larger whole, the essay. One essay may have many different kinds of well-developed paragraphs or combinations of paragraphs.

The structure of an essay is much like that of a paragraph, except that an essay is made up of many paragraphs. An essay usually has three parts: the introduction (beginning), the body (middle), and the conclusion (end). The introduction and conclusion will each be at least one paragraph, but the body will be many paragraphs. Each paragraph in the body will have a topic idea and will expand upon the essay's main idea (called the *thesis*) using appropriate supporting materials: examples and details, illustration, facts, statistics, or description.

As you read the following paragraph, notice the sentences that support the topic idea. What kind of supporting materials are used?

Topic sentence Even though medical students study very hard in school, they need to have additional skills to perform successful operations and become suc-
First cessful surgeons. <u>First</u>, they must learn to examine patients thoroughly
Next and check their illness records. <u>Next</u>, they need to have a lot of practice. Operations require great skill and speed of performance, which come only
Last with practice. <u>Last</u>, surgeons must watch their patients carefully in case there are post-operative complications. Only by doing these three things consistently will surgeons perform operations successfully.

The following essay expands the three points made in the paragraph. Notice how each point is discussed in further detail in the supporting paragraphs.

How to Be a Good Surgeon

Introduction Those who decide to become surgeons have to consider the many extra years of study beyond the bachelor's degree when they will learn the skills of their chosen specialty. Even though medical students spend many years and do a lot of hard work in medical school, they still have a lot to learn.
Thesis statement In order to become successful surgeons, doctors continue to learn in an ongoing process working with patients.
Topic sentence It is critical that doctors check the general health condition of their patients before surgery. Once nurses and technicians have checked the patients' blood pressure and heart condition and given the necessary

blood tests, doctors need to get the patients' past medical records and order any special tests that might be required. After they understand their patients' health condition well, doctors can decide what kind of operation to perform. Otherwise, the operation may be a failure.

Topic sentence   To be good surgeons, doctors have to be extremely skillful, so they must practice constantly. Operations need to be performed quickly and correctly to be successful. Some patients can't stand long periods under anesthesia. For them, operations have to be completed in the shortest time possible. This requires surgeons who are skillful and fast, so good surgeons are those who have practiced over and over to develop skills.

Topic sentence   Monitoring the patient after the operation will also help doctors succeed in saving people's lives. After the operation, some patients may have symptoms that forecast impending danger. Surgeons should continuously examine their patients, and, with the help of monitoring equipment and duty nurses, make diagnoses and give the patients further treatment if necessary.

Conclusion   It is obvious that doctors never stop learning, even after finishing their formal education. Examining all patients carefully, practicing surgical techniques frequently, and watching patients closely help surgeons continue to learn and become successful.

In this essay, the writer's main idea is stated in the introduction in the *thesis statement* (the main idea of the essay), referred to indirectly again in each paragraph through the *topic sentences,* and stated again in the *conclusion.* In each paragraph of the body the topic sentence supports the main idea or thesis statement, and each paragraph is further developed with examples.

Like a paragraph, an essay develops a main idea or point of view, but the discussion of each idea is much more extended. On the next page is a visual representation of an essay.

Introduction

Thesis Statement

Body

Supporting Paragraph

Topic Sentence

Supporting Sentences

Supporting Paragraph

Topic Sentence

Supporting Sentences

Supporting Paragraph

Topic Sentence

Supporting Sentences

Conclusion

As you write essays, present your ideas in a clear organizational pattern to help a reader understand your thoughts.

Preliminary Work

Your teacher has just given you a writing assignment. How will you begin? Will you jump right in and begin to write? Will you spend some time talking to others about your topic? Will you do some planning before you write?

Whatever your first language, you probably have a way of writing that is comfortable for you. No matter what method you use, this chapter will offer guidelines for developing composition skills. You will experience a writing process that can help you become a more fluent, versatile writer.

Limiting a Topic

After choosing a topic and gathering any necessary information, you must limit the topic you have chosen to develop it adequately. What does this mean?

A limited topic is a topic of manageable size. If a topic is too large, you can write only in generalizations and won't be able to use adequate description, examples, illustrations, or other forms of support that are necessary for good paragraphs. A paper with more depth and detail is much more interesting to a reader than a paper written in general terms.

Suppose you have decided to write about the general topic "Olympic Games." How could you limit this topic?

Here is an example:

- **Olympic Games**
- **Summer Games/Winter Games**
- **Events** in the summer Olympic Games
- **Track** as one event in the summer Olympic Games
- **Track** as one event in the summer Olympic Games in **Barcelona, Spain**.

In each case the topic is more and more limited, until a topic of manageable size is found. In the last item, the topic is limited to one event, in one season, and in one place.

Look at the following pairs of sentences to see how sentences 1 and 2 differ. One sentence in each pair clearly deals with a more limited topic. Which one is it?

A. Topic: food
1. Food additives are harmful.
2. Sodium nitrate, a food additive, is harmful to one's health.

B. Topic: pets
1. Pets need supervision, frequent health check-ups, and vaccinations.
2. Pets need care.

C. Topic: computers
1. Computers are used effectively for college registration.
2. Computers are used effectively for registration at Hilldale College.

D. Topic: war
1. War is destructive.
2. The war in Vietnam killed thousands of people, ruined the land for agriculture, and destroyed the economy of the country.

E. Topic: television
1. The National Geographic specials on TV are educational.
2. TV is educational.

Exercise 1. Comparing Topics

Three topic statements are given in each group. Of the three, which is the most limited? Rank the topics from least to most limited using numbers: 3 (least limited) 2 (less limited) 1 (most limited).

1. _____ Shakespeare wrote many plays that still entertain people today.

   _____ Shakespeare's *Hamlet,* written in 1542, entertains audiences with its tragic theme and dramatic style.

   _____ Shakespeare's *Hamlet,* written in 1542, still entertains people today.

2. _____ Soccer is popular in South America for a varety of reasons.

   _____ Sports are popular in South America for a variety of reasons.

   _____ Team sports are popular in South America for a variety of reasons.

3. _____ Inflation in Brazil affects all citizens in many ways.

_____ Inflation, a problem in many places around the world, has many effects on people's personal lives.

_____ Inflation in Brazil is causing people to have less and less spendable income to buy personal necessities.

4. _____ Everyone can enjoy the entertainment and challenge of board games.

_____ Everyone can enjoy the hours of entertainment that a game like chess can offer.

_____ Everyone can enjoy the entertainment and intellectual challenge of chess.

5. _____ Feelings and emotions can affect a person's ability to recover from illness.

_____ Cancer victims who have a positive outlook often succeed in surviving their fatal illness.

_____ Medical research has shown that emotions such as hope, faith, love, and laughter can help a person combat serious illness.

Exercise 2. Limiting Topics

Think about each of the following broad topics. One general sentence about the topic is provided. Write a second, more limited sentence. The words in parentheses may help you to think of a sentence. Use the sentences in Exercise 1 as models.

1. Solar energy

Solar energy is useful. (How?)

_____

2. Drugs

Drugs are harmful. (What kind of drugs?)

_____

3. Education

The government of a country has responsibility to provide education. (What kind and for whom?)

_____

4. Housing

Finding an apartment is difficult. (What about it is difficult?)

_____

5. Teachers

I have had some bad teachers. (When? Where?)

_____

6. Cities

Living in cities is stimulating. (In what way?)

_____

Clarifying Your Purpose

After limiting a topic, you are ready to work on a thesis statement. The thesis statement, similar to the topic sentence of a paragraph, expresses the author's idea or opinion. As you write this sentence, you must think about *why you are writing, whom you are writing for, and what you want to tell your readers.*

A limitless number of thesis statements may be written on any single topic, depending on the writer's purpose. You might want to define a term, summarize a point of view, explain a cause or effect, compare or contrast opposing viewpoints, all for the same topic. Writing a *statement of purpose* is one step in the process of writing a thesis statement.

Here are some statements of purpose written by students for papers in college courses on the topic, "Automobiles." For which college courses might these be written?

■ To show how the choice of a car reflects the owner's personality.

■ To show how the invention of the automobile changed American life.

■ To show how Japanese car manufacturers have forced changes to come about in the U.S. automobile industry.

■ To demonstrate the way advertisers compete to sell their automobile models.

Exercise 3. Writing Statements of Purpose

Write three possible statements of purpose for each of the following topics. Make sure your statements have been sufficiently limited so that you could write a short essay on each. Use a phrase beginning with "To show," "To tell," etc. One statement of purpose for the topic "health" has been given as an example.

1. Health
    a. *To tell how to increase your heart rate while jogging.*
    b. _____
    c. _____

2. Career choices
    a. _____
    b. _____
    c. _____

3. Public transportation
    a. _____
    b. _____
    c. _____

4. Modern technology
    a. _____
    b. _____
    c. _____

5. Television
    a. _____
    b. _____
    c. _____

Writing the Thesis Statement

Limiting a topic and clarifying your purpose are important first steps before writing the single sentence that summarizes and introduces an essay, the *thesis statement*. The thesis statement controls what is written and suggests how to present the material. The body of the essay itself supports the thesis statement.

A good thesis statement has the following characteristics.

1. *It is a complete sentence expressing a thought and usually does not begin with an interrogative word.* "My college is the best in the area in student achievement" rather than "Why my college is the best in the New York area."

2. *It limits the writer's idea to a manageable size.* "New York State sales taxes are unnecessarily high" is more limited than "Taxes are unnecessarily high."

3. *It often indicates the writer's opinion or purpose rather than stating an indisputable fact.* Thus, it is frequently an idea that can be disagreed with.

"Because cigarettes cause diseases, pollute the air, and annoy non-smokers, they should be banned from public places" is workable. "Cigarettes are expensive" is not.

4. *It should not give the writer's intention directly.* "Most people from my country share two common characteristics: friendly personalities and fierce national pride" would be better than "I am going to tell you about people from my country."

Look back at the introduction to the essay, "How to Be a Good Surgeon," at the beginning of this chapter. Note the thesis statement. Does it have these four characteristics?

Exercise 4. Evaluating Thesis Statements

Examine the sentences below. Using the preceding set of characteristics, explain why they may or may not be suitable as thesis sentences for short essays. Suggest how any of the unsuitable sentences could be improved.

1. I am going to tell you why I chose to move to the United States.
2. Unemployment rose 5 percent last year.
3. The importance of physical education classes in school.
4. American cars compared to European cars.
5. To produce a good picture, a photographer must pay attention to composition, color, and lighting.
6. Why should children in school have daily homework?
7. A nutritious diet is important.
8. Some people like to live in cities because of the social activities that are available, while others live there because there is more opportunity for employment.

The kind of thesis statement that is most effective will depend on your purpose. If it is to express your *opinion* and convince a reader of its validity, the thesis statement will reflect your opinion. If your purpose is to show how to do something or explain a *process*, the thesis will introduce that process.

If you examine the work of professional writers, you may have difficulty finding one sentence that expresses the thesis statement. Experienced writers often put their thesis idea in two or more sentences. Sometimes, in fact, they merely *imply* the controlling idea without expressing it in one particular sentence. As a beginning essay writer, however, you should always include a thesis statement in your introductory paragraph. This statement helps you to give a focus and unity to your essay.

Exercise 5. Selecting Thesis Statements

A topic, a statement of purpose, and two thesis statements are given. Select the thesis statement that best reflects the purpose for writing.

1. Topic: Sports

   Purpose: To explain why walking is good for people.

   Thesis: (a) Walking has many benefits, both physical an emotional.

   (b) Walking is a popular sport that everyone can enjoy.

2. Topic: Music

   Purpose: To show why the Santa Fe Opera has such a good reputation.

   Thesis: (a) The opera house in Santa Fe is the most beautiful building I have ever seen.

   (b) The Santa Fe Opera, which attracts young singers and the best musicians and directors, deserves its excellent reputation.

3. Topic: Transportation

   Purpose: To show why we should use more bicycles for city travel.

   Thesis: (a) Bicycles are the most dangerous vehicles to ride on heavily traveled highways.

   (b) Using bicycles instead of cars in cities would help solve the problem of pollution and over-crowded highways.

4. Topic: Aging

   Purpose: To show the problems of retired citizens in the U.S.

   Thesis: (a) When people retire, they often become inactive mentally and physically, have financial problems, and are lonely.

   (b) Retired citizens don't have very interesting lives.

5. Topic: Pets

   Purpose: To show that dogs are better than cats as pets.

   Thesis: (a) Every intelligent person knows that the best pet in the world is a dog.

   (b) Dogs make better pets than cats because they are smarter, more affectionate, and more helpful to their owners.

Exercise 6. Writing Statements of Purpose

A topic and thesis statement are given. Decide what the writer's purpose is, and write it on the line provided. Remember to use statements beginning with "To tell" or "To show." The first one is done for you.

1. Topic: Libraries

   Purpose: *To tell how a librarian can help you get started on a research paper.*

   Thesis: If you don't know where to start when you have to write a research paper for a class, just ask a librarian.

2. Topic: Male/female roles

   Purpose: _____

   Thesis: Male/female roles have changed radically in the United States since World War II.

3. Topic: Business

   Purpose: _____

   Thesis: The stock market is a very complex part of the business world, and individual investors need to know how it functions.

4. Topic: Air pollution

   Purpose: _____

   Thesis: Air pollution is a problem in many parts of the world these days, and it has serious effects on our health.

5. Topic: Medicine

   Purpose: _____

   Thesis: Lasers have been developed for doing complicated eye surgery that could not have been done even 20 years ago.

6. Topic: Education

   Purpose: _____

   Thesis: Some countries fail to meet the needs of the population for higher education.

Exercise 7. Writing Thesis Statements

A topic and a statement of purpose are given. Write a clear thesis statement. Remember the characteristics of a good thesis statement.

1. Topic: Housing

   Purpose: To show how public housing can help alleviate the economic burden of poor people.

   Thesis: _____

   _____

2. Topic: Education

   Purpose: To show the advantages of learning English.

   Thesis: _____

   _____

3. Topic: Entertainment

   Purpose: To show why people like to watch TV.

   Thesis: _____

   _____

4. Topic: Environment

   Purpose: To talk about how deforestation affects our environment.

   Thesis: _____

   _____

5. Topic: Health

   Purpose: To explain some of the problems caused by poor diet.

   Thesis: _____

   _____

Writing the Introduction

The introduction to an essay is important. It can either attract attention so that the reader continues to read or cause the reader to lose interest and stop, so it requires care and attention. How ideas are introduced depends on the audience and the type of essay. Every introduction should

- capture the reader's attention,
- present the main idea (thesis statement),
- give the reader an idea of what material will follow,
- hint at how the writing is organized.

Many writers have trouble writing introductions. Knowing some frequently used types is helpful. Introductions can include anecdotes, definitions, quotations, and humorous statements, but perhaps the most useful are those in the following examples.

Factual statements or historical background:

Health care practitioners are very concerned about one of the fastest growing health problems today, Alzheimer's disease, which robs elderly people of memory. Experts say that about 10 percent of people over age 65 and 47 percent of people over 85 suffer from this disease. Health planners are alarmed by these figures. The number of people over 85 is growing fast, and by the year 2050, more than 14 million Americans might have the disease. Since doctors don't know what causes it, and they have no cure, there is a real question of how to solve this growing health problem.

A brief description:

We climbed in the ski lift to go to the top of the Aguille du Midi, a mountain high above the town of Chamonix, France, before the sun was up. The air was clear and fresh at dawn, and the sun began to shine behind the mountain ahead of us. From the windows of the small ski lift, we could see the jagged rocks under us and the top of the awesome peak above us. All twenty of us in the group were excitedly looking forward to our first ski trip on a glacier down the back side of the mountain, an experience we would never forget.

The narration of an incident:

In 1984, as I was traveling across the United States with a college friend, our car broke down in a small town in Kansas. It was a weekend, and we couldn't get the car repaired for several days. Trying to save money, we had been taking turns driving day and night and didn't want to pay for a hotel room. When we told the garage attendant, he offered us a room on his farm at the edge of town. It was during those three days with a farm family in a small town in Kansas that I learned how friendly Americans can be.

A question:

Have you ever entered a room that was filled with people you had never met? How did you feel? What did you do? Most people in such a situation rely on the skill of "small talk." Just what is "small talk"? It is pleasant talk about rather unimportant matters. Some people don't like small talk. They would rather share deep thoughts. However, for most of us, small talk about things such as the weather, family matters, jobs, hobbies, sports, or school is a way of relaxing and getting to meet new friends.

A shared experience:

The English language is plagued with the most erratic spelling practices of all the great languages. This fact needs little introduction, especially to those of us who have tried to learn English as a second or foreign language. Even native speakers of the language have trouble with its spelling irregularities, which are a result of four principal factors: the historical development of spelling in English; the advent of printing; the resistance of the established spelling to change with phonetic change; and the nature of the English language to borrow and accept words from other languages.

Many introductions begin with background information of a general type and lead to the thesis by a combination of the methods presented above. Can you identify the techniques used in the following introduction?

Almost everyone in the United States has been to a McDonald's restaurant. Whether you like the hamburgers or not, you must admit that McDonald's cannot be ignored as part of the American restaurant scene. Why is it so popular? Almost one-third of all hamburgers sold in U.S. restaurants are sold in McDonald's. In fact, its sales are larger than the combined sales of Pizza Hut, Burger King, and Kentucky Fried Chicken. A new McDonald's opens every 15 hours somewhere in the world, so wherever you go, you might run into one. There are now almost 11,000 McDonald's, one-fourth of which are in foreign countries. A brief look at the development of this restaurant chain may explain its overwhelming popularity.

Exercise 8. Writing Introductions

For each of the following introductions, define the type of material used (factual statements, historical background, description, narration, questions, shared experience), the thesis statement, and the purpose for writing. Remember: an introduction may include a variety of methods.

1. Have you ever had a headache, backache, or sore muscles? Of course you have, and perhaps you have taken aspirin, gone to a doctor, or visited your chiropractor, but have you ever considered acupuncture? This traditional Chinese method of treatment might help you. However, you might like to know something about the philosophy, background, and methodology of acupuncture before you consider treatment.

   Method:_____

   Thesis statement:_____

   _____

   Purpose: to _____

   _____

2. More Americans now face housing problems than at any other time since the 1930s. According to an expert at Harvard University, house prices and interest rates have risen four times faster than the real incomes people have had to spend. In 1991 the average price of a new one-family home was $120,000. At this rate, not only the poor and the elderly on fixed incomes but also the middle-class have problems buying a new home. There is also a problem with rents, especially in the West and Northeast, where prices have soared. The number of homeless people on the streets of many American cities is further evidence of the problem. In the future, people will be looking for ways to solve the housing problem. The government and nonprofit groups will have to become more active in helping to make home ownership easier through support with federal funds and tax incentives.

Method: _____

Thesis statement: _____

_____

Purpose: to _____

_____

3. Flying over the Potomac River to land at National Airport on our first trip to Washington, D.C, we saw the tip of the Washington Monument surrounded by rolling green lawns and hundreds of multi-colored kites blowing high in the breezes. Off to the south, we could see the Jefferson Memorial and to the west, the Lincoln Memorial and the Reflecting Pool. Washington, D.C., a beautiful and entertaining city, has many lovely sights to offer a tourist.

Method: _____

Thesis statement: _____

_____

Purpose: to _____

_____

4. About the year 221 B.C., a great emperor named Shih Huang Ti united different parts of China into an empire. North of his empire lived barbaric wanderers of the desert lands, and he felt they were a danger to his empire, so he ordered that a great wall be built to protect all the northern provinces. This Great Wall of China was a tremendous project, and it was completed in only fifteen years. Did

the emperor accomplish his goal with the Great Wall? A review of history will answer this question.

Method:_____

Thesis statement:_____

_____

Purpose: to _____

_____

STRUCTURE REVIEW: Clause Structures

Chapter One discussed *independent clauses,* structures that have a subject and a verb and can stand alone as a sentence.

> Medical scientists continue to work on cancer research.

Conjunctions and sentence connectors join independent clauses that could stand alone without being connected.

> Medical scientists continue to work on cancer research, <u>and</u> it is hoped that some day a cure will be found.

Combining such sentences (coordination) is a way to make cohesive connections between ideas.

Subordination is another way of connecting ideas, but instead of connecting two independent clauses, one independent clause and one dependent clause are joined. *Dependent clauses* are structures that have a subject and a verb but cannot stand alone as a sentence. For example, a student walks into your classroom and says only:

> When class is finished… (dependent clause)

Would you understand? Would you want to ask some questions? What does the student plan to do after class? The clause standing alone expresses only part of an idea. It needs something added to make the idea complete.

> When class is finished, let's go to the cafeteria.

The first part of the sentence (the dependent clause) has to have the second part (the independent clause) to be complete.

The two types of dependent clauses discussed in this lesson are *adverbial* and *adjective* clauses. Just like structures of coordination, structures of subordination are important ways to add *coherence* to writing. A text has coherence when the ideas are linked in some logical manner to help the reader understand the relationship between them.

Adverbial Clauses

Two ideas can be combined with a subordinating conjunction to show the relationship between them. These relationships and some of the more common subordinating conjunctions appear in the following list.

Type of relationship	*Common subordinating conjunctions*
Cause/reason	because, since
Condition	if, unless, provided (that), as long as
Time	when, before, after, as, since, whenever, while, until
Place	where, wherever
Contrast/concession	although, though, even though, even if, whether or not, while
Purpose/result	so (that), in order (that)
Manner	as if, as though

In the following sentences with adverbial clauses, the emphasis is on the idea in the independent clause. The adverbial clause (the part beginning with the subordinating conjunction) adds related but secondary information. In these examples, what do you notice about the punctuation?

Cause	Bob was late today *because he missed the bus.*
Condition	*If you go with me,* I will attend the meeting.
Time	*While we are waiting,* let's have a cup of tea.
Place	Let's have the dance *where it was held last year.*
Concession	He ate the cake *although he dislikes chocolate.*
Contrast	*While Mary is an optimist,* her twin brother is a pessimist.
Purpose	He got a job *so that he could pay his tuition.*
Manner	He talked on the phone *as if he were angry.*

Exercise 1. Adverbial Clauses

Complete the following adverbial clauses, expressing the relationship between the two clauses indicated by the subordinating conjunction. Be sure to use a *clause* and not just a time phrase on numbers 4 and 6. The first is done for you.

1. Because *he refused to study enough,* John did not pass the exam.

2. The little child refused to eat the food her mother gave her even though _____.

3. As long as _____, you can continue to be an employee here.

4. My brother will be at the university until _____ _____.

5. The office will be open whenever _____.

6. Martin had already finished dinner before _____.

7. Please carry the box carefully so that _____.

8. Unless _____, you will not understand the professor's lecture.

9. While some of the students _____, others worked in groups.

10. We can have the party wherever _____.

Exercise 2. Subordinating Conjunctions in a Paragraph

Fill in the blanks, using adverbs (or subordinating conjunctions) of the type indicated. Refer to the chart on p. 44 if necessary.

Where did the Native Americans come from? _____ (concession) many tales from among Native American Indian tribes trace their origins to the North American continent, most scholars accept the theory that the Native Americans came to the Western Hemisphere from Asia. They believe that _____ (time) they crossed the Bering Strait from Asia, they began to spread across the continent. _____ (contrast) the dates of their immigration aren't yet established, some evidence suggests 80,000 years ago. The nomadic people who crossed from Siberia to Alaska came _____ (purpose) they could follow the animals that they hunted. They survived here by living in harmony with the land. _____ (time) the Europeans arrived in 1492, there were about 1,115,000 indigenous Native American people on the continent. These Americans welcomed the whites, but _____ (cause) they were so different, the Europeans thought they were uncivilized. By 1890, there were fewer than 90,000 Native Americans. They had lost their lives, lands, religion, and language to the newer immigrants.

Conditional Clauses

Conditional or "if" clauses describe a condition. The action of the independent clause depends on this condition. Conditional clauses are often used in writing about a process (which you will do in the next chapter).

For example, in describing methods for frying an egg, you might say, "If you like your egg 'sunny-side up,' allow it to cook in the pan without turning it. However, if you like the yolk browned, turn the egg once after the white becomes solid."

Each of the different types of conditional clauses in English expresses a different meaning and is used for a different purpose. Combinations of verb tenses express time in a way that is different from usual verb usage. Conditional forms fall into two categories: "real" and "unreal."

Real Conditions

Real conditions in the present time express a habitual action. Both verbs are in the simple present form. When used, the word *if* has the meaning *whenever.*

In fact, *whenever* is often used instead of *if.*

> If (whenever) I wake up late, I am late to school.

> If (whenever) I am late to school, the teacher marks me absent.

Real conditions in the future time express an action that may or may not occur in the future.* They are often used to make predictions. The verb in the *if* clause is in the present form, and *will* is used with the verb in the independent clause. *May* and *can* are also sometimes used. Notice

---

*Real conditions are sometimes used in the past time to express a habitual action or a general situation that occurred in the past. Both verbs are in the simple past tense.

If I woke up late, I was late to school. (when I was a child)

If I was late to school, the teacher marked me absent.

(Again, *if* means *whenever.*)

that the *if* clause may be at the beginning or at the end of the sentence. What happens to the punctuation?

> If you study hard, you will pass the course.
>
> You will do well on the test if you take good notes.
>
> If you work hard, you can pass this course easily.

Unless is often used in real conditions. It has the meaning of *if not*. Notice what happens in the three examples given when the word *unless* is substituted for *if*:

> Unless you study hard, you will not pass this course.
>
> You will not do well on the test unless you take good notes.
>
> Unless you work hard, you cannot pass this course easily.

Exercise 3. Completing Sentences with Real Conditions in the Present

Complete the following sentences by stating what is always true for students under the given conditions. What verb forms should you use?

1. If students plan their time well, _____.

2. If international students practice speaking English daily,

   _____.

3. _____ if teachers give easy tests.

4. _____ if teachers don't speak clearly and slowly.

5. Students have a hard time in school if _____.

6. Unless you change the oil in your car regularly, _____

   _____.

7. _____ unless we hurry.

8. Unless children receive discipline at home, _____

   _____.

Exercise 4. Completing Sentences with Real Conditions in the Future

Complete the following sentences, in which you give advice to a friend about his or her health. What verb form should you use?

1. If you brush your teeth regularly, _____.

2. If you exercise regularly, _____.

3. _____ if you stop smoking.

4. If you eat a lot of junk food, _____.

5. If _____, you will probably have to see a
   doctor.

Unreal Conditions

Unreal conditions in the present time can be used to express situations that
don't exist at the present time. They are often used to make wishes and
to give advice. The verb in the *if* clause is in the past form, and *would* is
used in the independent clause. *Might* and *could* are also used. If the verb
to be is used in the *if* clause, *were* is used for all subjects.

> If Mahatma Gandhi were alive, I would go to hear him speak.
>
> (He is not alive, so I cannot hear him.)
>
> If I were an American, I would already speak English well.
>
> (I am not an American, so I must study English now.)
>
> If I were rich, I would buy my friends gifts.
>
> (I am not rich. I wish I were.)

Unreal conditions in the past time refer to a situation that didn't occur.
They are often used to discuss past mistakes as a result of something not
happening or to make apologies for something in the past. The *past perfect* verb form and *would have* + the verb are used. *Could have* and *might
have* are also used.

> If I had been alive in the 1940s, I would have heard a lot about World
>   War II.
>
> (I wasn't born yet.)
>
> If I hadn't failed that second test, I would have passed the course.
>
> (I failed that second test.)

Unreal conditions in past/present time make an "unreal" statement about
the past that has a result in the present time. The verb in the *if* clause is
in the *past perfect form* to express the unreal condition in the past time.
Would is used in the main clause to express a present result.

> If the South had won the Civil War, the United States would be different
>   today.
>
> (The South didn't win.)
>
> If I had been born in 1925, I would be retired now.
>
> (I wasn't born in 1925.)

Exercise 5. Completing Sentences with Unreal Conditions in the Present

Complete the following sentences to express what you would do under the different conditions. What verb forms will you use?

1. I don't have my own car. If I did, _____

   _____.

2. I don't have my own computer. If I did, _____

   _____.

3. I am a very busy person. If I weren't so busy, _____

   _____.

4. I have a small house/apartment. If it were larger, _____

   _____.

5. I am not a scientist. If I were, _____

   _____.

Complete the following sentences to express the conditions under which you would do the following. What verb forms will you use?

6. I might take a trip to Hawaii if _____

   _____.

7. I would have people over to visit every day if _____

   _____.

8. I would spend my time reading books if _____

   _____.

9. My boss would probably fire me if _____

   _____.

10. The world would be a peaceful place if _____

    _____.

Exercise 6. Completing Sentences with Unreal Conditions in the Past

Complete the following sentences, telling how your life would have been different in the past under the given conditions. What verb forms will you use?

1. If my parents had never met, _____.

2. If I hadn't learned to read in the first grade, _____.

3. If I had been born a girl/boy, _____.

4. If I hadn't finished high school, _____.

Exercise 7. Completing Sentences with Unreal Conditions in the Past and Present

Complete the following sentences, telling how life would be different today if certain things had not happened in the past. Be sure to write *present* rather than past consequences.

1. If computers hadn't been invented, _____.

2. If I hadn't graduated from high school, _____.

3. If penicillin had not been discovered, _____.

4. If Hitler hadn't been born, _____.

Adjective Clauses

Adjective clauses, another kind of dependent clause used to join ideas, are used as modifiers.

> The player *who made the goal* was elated.

What are the characteristics of adjective clauses?

■ They usually begin with a relative pronoun (*who, whom, whose, which, that*) and sometimes with a relative adverb (*where* or *when*) or a phrase including a pronoun (*some of which, a few of whom*).

■ Sometimes these pronouns can be omitted.

■ They always follow a noun and modify (describe or limit) that noun.

■ They are punctuated according to specific rules.

How are adjective clauses used?

To describe a person:

> The soccer players *who played on the school team* were all from South America.

> The goalie *whom I told you about* came from Brazil.

To describe a place:

> The field *where they played* was in an old school yard.

To describe a thing:

> The uniforms *(that) they wore* were colorful.

The bleachers, *some of which were broken*, were always full of spectators.

To define time:

In 1989, *when the team won the championship,* scouts from national teams began to come to the games.

To show possession:

The player *whose head-ball scored the winning goal* was elated.

How are adjective clauses punctuated?

When using adjective clauses, a writer has to make decisions about punctuation. Sometimes an adjective clause just gives additional information about an already specific noun.

New York City, *which is the largest city in the United States*, is famous for its nightlife.

The TOEFL exam, *which is a requirement for most universities*, is given all around the world.

Sometimes a clause is essential to define or specify a particular noun.

The city *where I grew up* was small compared to New York.

The exam *(that) we took for placement into English classes* lasted about two hours.

Compare the preceding two sets of sentences that have adjective clauses. What is the rule for punctuation?

When do you use *that* and when do you use *which*?

When a clause is essential, the pronoun *that* is used in place of *which.*

The house *that* we bought was designed by a famous architect.

That cannot be used in a nonessential clause. Relative pronouns may be omitted in essential clauses when the pronouns are objects of verbs or prepositions.

Incorrect   The White House, *that* is the home of all U.S. presidents, was designed by James Hoban, who won an architecture competition.

Correct   The White House, *which* is the home of all U.S. presidents, was designed by James Hoban, who won an architecture competition.

That cannot be omitted when it is the subject of the clause.

Incorrect   The house won the architecture competition was designed by my uncle.

Correct   The house *that* won the architecture competition was designed by my uncle.

Exercise 8. Pronouns and Adverbs

Fill in the blanks with *who(m), that, which, or where.* As you do the exercise, notice how the clauses are punctuated.

Where did the word *hamburger* come from? According to authorities, it started on the Russian Steppes, _____ medieval Tartars ate raw meat _____ looked like our present-day hamburger. German sailors, _____ tasted the meat, took it home to a German city _____ was called Hamburg. The people there didn't like the raw meat, so they broiled the outside. German immigrants brought this "hamburger steak" to America, _____ it was introduced in a lunch wagon in New Haven, Connecticut, by Louis Lassen, _____ put it between two slices of bread. In 1904, at a great fair in St. Louis, hamburgers were introduced, along with ice cream and iced tea, to the American public.

Soon hamburger stands grew up all over the country as Americans became enamored with drive-in restaurants. In 1954, the McDonald brothers' hamburger stand, _____ stood between two golden arches in San Bernardino, California, was discovered by Ray Croc, _____ bought out the brothers and began to spread hamburger franchises all over the world. There are other hamburger franchises, but McDonalds', _____ sells some eight million hamburgers a day, is by far the largest.

Now, we are told that eating hamburgers can be hazardous to our health because of all of the food additives, some of _____ are even carcinogenic (cancer-causing). However, the food _____ began on the Steppes of Russia is as much a part of the American diet as hot dogs and apple pie.

Exercise 9. Using Adjective Clauses

Combine the following sentences, changing the second sentence into an adjective clause that modifies the underlined noun or noun phrase in the first sentence. Punctuate, and be prepared to explain your use of punctuation. Some sentences may have several possible combinations, and pronouns may sometimes be omitted. The first one has been done for you.

1. We hired <u>Ms. Jones</u>.
   We interviewed her yesterday.
   We hired Ms. Jones, whom we interviewed yesterday.

2. The <u>guests</u> had to fight a snow storm to come to the party.
   Some of them arrived very late.

   _____

3. <u>Arabic</u> is offered at this university.
   Arabic is a Semitic language.

   _____

4. The <u>police officer</u> warned me not to park here again.
   He works part-time for the university.

   _____

5. The <u>letters</u> must be signed today.
   The secretary has just typed the letters.

   _____

6. The <u>Watergate</u> became notorious during the Nixon administration.
   The Watergate is a complex of apartments, shops, and offices in Washington, D.C.

   _____

7. The treasure <u>chest</u> once belonged to Spanish pirates.
   The divers found gold in it.

   _____

8. The <u>suggestion</u> was accepted by the committee.
   You made the suggestion to increase the membership.

   _____

9. The <u>Rocky Mountains</u> can be treacherous to hikers in winter.
   The Rocky Mountains are a huge chain of mountains from Canada to Mexico.

   _____

10. The popular <u>author</u> was honored at a banquet.
    His book has just been published.

    _____

11. The <u>senator</u> is running for president.
    I voted for her in the last election.

_____

12. <u>China</u> has surpassed the mark of one billion inhabitants.
    It is the most populous country in the world.

_____

Exercise 10. Editing Adjective Clauses

Certain errors often occur when students begin to use adjective clauses in their writing. Some of the more common errors can be found in the following sentences. Read them to find any of these errors: verb agreement, use of pronouns or adverbs, missing prepositions, and punctuation. Discuss these errors with your teacher and correct them.

1. The young man who live next door is giving a graduation party.
2. The man is from France is a good musician.
3. The seat which I sat was very uncomfortable.
4. The teacher her books were stolen had to buy new ones.
5. The girl who I talked had just lost her job.
6. The house in where the family lives isn't large enough.
7. All the students which the teacher has graded their papers so far have failed the test.
8. That car which the police towed it last night was parked illegally.

Exercise 11. Sentence Combining

Use structures of coordination and subordination to join each pair of numbered sentences. Do not change unnumbered sentences. Write in paragraph form. (If you do not know what a bridal "train" is, find out before you write the last sentence!)

The groom stood nervously waiting for his bride.   *(1)* The church had been decorated with many flowers.   *(1)* It had a wonderful fragrance.   *(2)* The organ was playing.   *(2)* People were looking eagerly down the aisle.   *(3)* Suddenly the music changed.   *(3)* The bride appeared at the entrance to the church.   *(4)* The bride, who was a vision of beauty, held the arm of her father.   *(4)* He was smiling proudly.   *(5)* The bride's mother was filled with bittersweet happiness as she watched her daughter's entrance.   (5) The mother was dressed in a blue gown.

The young girls in the congregation sighed as they thought of their own wedding days.   (6) The bride knew she was the envy of all the girls. (6) She was graceful and confident.   (7) She arrived at the altar steps. (7) She tripped on the lace train flowing behind her and fell flat on her face!

WRITING ASSIGNMENT ONE:
Writing an Adventure Story Together

You are to create an adventure story with three or four of your classmates. Each of you will write one part of the story. Before you look at the directions for this assignment, read the following example of a group adventure story. It is written about King Arthur, a legendary king during the Middle Ages in Europe. The "Round Table" consisted of King Arthur's advisors, much like a modern day "cabinet." As you read, notice that at the end of each paragraph, there is a choice. The choice is made at the beginning of the next paragraph.

THE DRAGON'S CAVE

Sir Wonderful is a knight of King Arthur's Round Table. King Arthur has given the knight a "quest" (a task to be completed). Sir Wonderful must go to the countryside to fight and kill a dragon that has been terrorizing the peasants. Sir Wonderful may take with him his trusty horse, Valiant, his shield, and either a mighty sword or a magic bow and arrow. (CHOICE: Which weapon will Sir Wonderful take?)

Student 1. He selects the mighty sword. Sir Wonderful mounts Valiant and rides swiftly toward the dragon's cave. Nearing his destination, he comes upon bandits in the road who are robbing an old traveler. (CHOICE: Will Sir Wonderful stop to help the old man or will he continue swiftly on the quest given him by the King?)

Student 2. Sir Wonderful, who is noble and charitable, stops to help the old man. Threatening the robbers with death by his mighty sword, Sir Wonderful easily rescues the old man. The knight is astonished to discover that the traveler is none other than King Arthur's teacher and great friend, Merlin the Magician. In recognition of Sir Wonderful's kindness, Merlin places a magic spell upon the shield, making it so strong that it will protect Sir Wonderful from any blow. Sir Wonderful continues his journey and reaches the dragon's cave. (CHOICE: Will he enter or tell the dragon to come outside?)

Student 3. Knowing that the cave will be dark and dangerous, Sir Wonderful calls the dragon to come outside. Breathing fire and smoke, an enormous, scaly beast appears at the entrance to the cave. The monster approaches, whipping its enormous tail behind it. Fire almost burns Sir Wonderful. (CHOICE: Will the knight attack or retreat?)

Student 4 (or the whole group). Sir Wonderful is fearless and brave, so he attacks. Protecting himself from the fiery breath of the dragon with his shield, Sir Wonderful creeps beneath the beast. Everyone knows that the belly of a dragon is unprotected, so the knight aims his sword at the area around the dragon's heart. He strikes. With an awful roar, the dragon falls to the ground dead. The neighboring peasants, hearing the good news, prepare food and drink for a celebration in honor of Sir Wonderful, who has saved them from the terrible dragon.

Pre-Writing Exercise

1. With the class, brainstorm about possible variations in the story "The Dragon's Cave." How could the story have developed if the opposite choice had been made at the end of each paragraph?

2. As a class, look at how the story is written in the present tense. What effect does that have on the reader? Take turns reading the paragraphs aloud and at the same time changing the verbs to the past tense. Which do you prefer?

3. Practice a story with the class. The teacher will read one of the "Beginning Sentences" that follow and will call on different students to add one line to continue the story. Try to add action details and use colorful language as you develop the plot. When you think the story should end, add a concluding sentence.

4. Practice creating a story orally in a small group of students. Form a circle with three or four classmates. Choose one of the other "Beginning Sentences." Each student in the group should speak for two or three minutes to add to the story. The story can continue around the circle until one student thinks it is time to conclude. One person or the group can create the conclusion.

Beginning Sentences:

1. One night, during a fierce thunderstorm, all of the lights went out in town.

2. Tom Wilson received a telegram that delivered some surprising news.

3. We were driving down a lonely country road when our car suddenly broke down miles from any town or farmhouse.

4. Mr. and Mrs. Anderson had been asleep for several hours when they were awakened by suspicious noises.

5. We were sitting in class, listening to the teacher, when one student fainted and fell out of her chair.

Group Writing

Now that you have had some practice adding to stories orally, you are ready to do the group writing with several other students. The teacher may give you time in class to work on the story, or you may be asked to do it outside of class. It is important that each student in the group do his or her paragraph on time, since every paragraph depends on the one preceding it.

1. Select one of the beginning paragraphs (Adventure 1, Adventure 2, Adventure 3, Adventure 4) for your story.

2. Working one after the other, write one paragraph each. The first paragraph follows the introduction. The second paragraph follows the first one, and so on.

3. End each paragraph with a choice to be made. The beginning of the next paragraph indicates what choice was made (see the sample story).

4. Write the conclusion together.

5. Together, look over all the choices and paragraphs to make sure that all writers have made smooth transitions between the paragraphs and that

sentences have been connected to join ideas. (If your story has been done on the computer, each person should have a copy at this point.)

6. Edit your story for errors in spelling, punctuation, grammar, and sentence structure.

7. Write the final draft.

ADVENTURE 1: MOUNTAIN CLIMB

Three members of the college Hiking Club have decided to climb a good-sized mountain near the campus. They estimate that the climb will take five hours. They are leaving early in the morning and plan to return home before dark. It's a beautiful early spring day and the weather report is good, but freak snowstorms sometimes occur during this season. The hikers want to carry as little equipment as possible so that the climb will be easier. (CHOICE: Will they take extra food and blankets in case of emergency, or will they decide to travel light?)

ADVENTURE 2: TREASURE HUNT

Two fortune hunters have each managed to obtain one half of a map that gives directions to a great treasure. A 17th century pirate buried a chest of Spanish coins and jewelry on an island in the Caribbean. The two fortune hunters, Jake the Snake and One-eyed Bernie, know which island it is, but in order to find the exact location, they must either work together or try to get the other half of the map. Neither Jake nor Bernie is known for his honesty, and neither trusts the other. (CHOICE: Will Jake work with Bernie and share the treasure, or will he try to get the map himself?)

ADVENTURE 3: THE TIME MACHINE

Professor Wizard and his assistant, Gloria, have invented a marvelous machine that sends people into different periods of time. Now it is time to make the first experiment, and the professor and Gloria will send themselves on a voyage through time. They are not sure how well the machine will work, so they make out their wills and say farewell to their families and friends. The professor wants to go back to the past, but Gloria is curious about the future. They get into the "Time Machine" and are ready to set the date they will travel to. (CHOICE: Will they go into the past or select a future date?)

ADVENTURE 4: THE ENCHANTED FOREST

On a cool autumn morning, a beautiful princess named Diana (Di, for short) is walking in the forest near her castle looking for wildflowers. She has become distracted as she gathers an armful of blossoms and suddenly finds that she is in an unfamiliar part of the forest. In fact, she no longer recognizes the species of flowers she sees, the trees appear to be much taller, and strange-looking birds and animals appear and disappear. She must be in the part of the forest where elves and enchanted creatures live. She comes to a small bridge across a stream. To her left is a path with a strange light glowing at the end of it. (CHOICE: Will Diana cross the bridge or take the path?)

WRITING ASSIGNMENT TWO:

Writing a Narrative on Your Own

Your second assignment for this chapter is to write a narration, a story telling what happened in order of time.

For this assignment, choose a personal event that was painful, terrifying, rewarding, moving, or meaningful for you in some other way. Before you write, find a partner and relate your story. Let this classmate ask you questions as you speak. By answering the questions, you will see where to add more detail to your story.

Now listen to your partner's story and ask him or her questions.

After you have shared your experience and are ready to write, take these preliminary steps.

1. Write down your purpose for writing an essay on the topic. Remember to begin "To...."

   For example:

   > To narrate the story of my journey from my country to the United States and show how it helped me to mature.

2. Write a thesis statement in which what the event meant to you is clear. In other words, include a thesis statement that lets the reader know whether this event was terrifying, rewarding, joyful, educationally meaningful, etc. Your teacher and classmates can help you with this step after they have heard your story.

3. Write an introduction, choosing an appropriate method to suit your narrative.

4. Before writing the body of your narrative, think about how it will divide into paragraphs. Remember that paragraphs group related ideas together.

5. Exchange papers with your classmate for peer editing. Give each other suggestions for revision, such as changing the order of ideas or adding details.

6. Write a final draft of your narrative after considering your class-mate's suggestions. Use appropriate connecting words to join your ideas in sentences.

7. Edit your final draft for errors in spelling, punctuation, grammar, and sentence structure.

SUMMARY WRITING
Part Two: More Preparation for Summary Writing

In Chapter One, we practiced finding main ideas in short paragraphs and then choosing from possible restatements of those main ideas. Let's continue to practice choosing the best restatement of an author's main idea, remembering that in summary writing, we must restate the author's ideas in our own words.

Exercise 1. Restating Main Ideas

Read each paragraph and underline the main idea sentence. Then choose the sentence that best restates the main idea.

1. It has been found that many obese persons eat food to get satisfaction or to compensate for personality problems. An overweight girl who is not socially accepted may make herself feel better by eating rich desserts or junk foods. Persons who are tense, afraid, bored, or frustrated may find that eating makes them feel better. A person who lacks affection or recognition may also turn to food. There is evidence that psychological factors may play a role in obesity problems for many people.

_____ a. Obese people are not socially accepted.

_____ b. Overweight people may be tense or frustrated.

_____ c. Obesity may be influenced by psychological factors.

2. In the United States, formal education is not only freely available but also compulsory. American parents are legally obliged to send their children to school. However, they can choose between sending their children to public or private schools. Public education in the United States is financed by taxing everyone, even those people without children or those whose children attend private schools. Americans believe that public education benefits everyone in the society. Every child is thus entitled to get twelve years of schooling at public expense.

_____ a. Children can attend public or private schools.

_____ b. Public education is free in the United States, and every child must go to school.

_____ c. Public education is good for the whole society.

3. The memory unit of a computer is where information is stored. It is similar to a filing cabinet where both information for solving a problem and instructions on how to use the information are stored. Computer systems contain internal memory units for the storage of instructions and data; in addition, they may include external systems to increase the memory capacity and provide flexibility. Without this storage, the computer would have no heart.

_____ a. The heart of the computer is the memory unit.

_____ b. There are internal and external memory units.

_____ c. The memory unit of a computer is like a filing cabinet.

4. Being a good parent does not come automatically, and it is certainly not easy! To reduce pain, increase safety, and ensure the health of the newborn, many modern parents educate themselves about behavior and care during pregnancy and childbirth. Prospective parents should also take steps to learn effective parenting techniques. Reading about childhood development and behavior or attending classes on parenting can contribute to success and reduce the frustrations and anxieties that inevitably occur.

_____ a. Being a parent can be frustrating.

_____ b. Being a good parent involves training and effort.

_____ c. Good parenting is quickly achieved by most people.

5. Many people complain about not being able to remember names when they meet people for the first time, but memory experts tell us that there are rules to follow and tricks to use. First, be sure that you hear the name clearly when the person is introduced to you. If you don't, ask that the name be repeated. Next, ask how the name is spelled; you will be sure that you have understood it then. Another aid is to try to make some remark about the name, such as, "Oh, I once had a teacher by that name!" Also, try to use the name appropriately throughout the conversation and use it again when you say goodbye. All of these suggestions will help you to remember names, but the best way is to try to visualize something tangible that the name makes you think of or to relate the name in some way to the person's face. Can you think of a way that a person meeting you for the first time could remember your name?

_____ a. A lot of people have trouble remembering names.

_____ b. Experts suggest several ways to help us remember names the first time we hear them.

_____ c. Using a name over and over in a conversation can help you to remember it.

6. In the 1980s, little known to anyone, an important milestone was reached in the United States. The number of pizza restaurants exceeded the number of hamburger restaurants! It is obvious that pizza is very popular, but where did it all begin? Most people believe that the pizza began in Naples, Italy, where around the year 1000, a circle of dough covered with herbs and spices was called *picea.* Around the year 1500, when explorers brought the tomato from the newly-discovered Americas, pizza took on a new look. In 1889, a restaurant owner in Naples was asked to prepare a pie for the queen. He made a pizza with the colors of the Italian flag: tomato for the red, basil for the green, and mozzarella cheese for the white, the ingredients of the modern pizza. In 1905, the first pizzeria opened in New York City, and pizza could generally be found in Italian neighborhoods. Later, because of the requests of returning World War II GIs, who had gotten a taste for pizza in Italy, the demand for pizza began to spread. In 1958, the first Pizza Hut opened in Wichita, Kansas, and now millions of people eat at some 5,000 Pizza Huts in the United States.

_____ a. Pizza, which has a long history, is fast replacing the hamburger as America's favorite food.

_____ b. The first pizza was believed to have been made in Naples, Italy.

_____ c. American GIs helped to spread the demand for pizza in the United States.

Exercise 2. Finding and Writing Main Ideas

This exercise will give you practice writing main ideas. Read each paragraph carefully. As you read, underline any sentence(s) you think contain the main ideas of the paragraph. (Remember, the main idea is not always the first sentence and may be found in more than one sentence!) In your own words, write the main idea on the lines provided.

1. In the morning, the city of Washington, D.C., is full of action and excitement. People in the White House, on Capitol Hill, and in government departments and offices are working nonstop to decide what is best for the United States. However, when the afternoon rush hour passes and night arrives, the dangerous face of the city appears. You can seldom find anyone at 10:00 p.m. walking down Constitution Avenue, the busiest avenue in the Washington metropolitan area during the day. This is partly because the government offices are closed, but even more because a lot of people are afraid of the danger. Even the prosperous northwestern

part of the city, including Georgetown's famous nightlife area, is not free of this danger. A classic crime in Washington is committed by muggers who might kill a victim if he doesn't have enough cash to satisfy the robbers. Taxi drivers are often the victims of such violent crimes when they drive in downtown Washington at night. Danger is always lurking in the nation's capital after dark, so many people don't go in certain areas downtown after working hours.

Main Idea _____

_____

_____

2. The term "funny bone" is very odd. The "funny bone" is the commonly used expression for the bone of the upper part of the arm, from the elbow to the shoulder. Anyone who has ever accidentally hit his or her elbow sharply against a hard surface will sympathize with my sister Rachel and her complaint. Yesterday, she struck her "funny bone" against the corner of a door and felt a great deal of pain. When I laughed and said, "Oh, you hit your funny bone!" she replied that there was nothing "funny" about it. She wondered why such an odd name was given to this particular part of the body. Then I explained to her that the scientific name for this bone is the "humerus," which is a homonym for "humorous," meaning "funny." This is just one instance of odd expressions that can be explained by examining their origins or earlier meanings.

Main Idea _____

_____

_____

3. There are many different kinds of addictions. The type most people think of immediately is alcoholism. People who cannot stop drinking until they become intoxicated have an addiction that is usually as much physical as psychological. Another example is an addiction to gambling. Some people are so drawn to the possibility of "striking it rich" that they gamble even their rent and food budget and become penniless in their search for fortune. Another type of addictive behavior is overeating. To compensate for some psychological problem in their lives, some people eat much more than needed to satisfy their hunger. Even though they aren't in the least hungry, they can't resist reaching for one more slice of pizza or piece of cake. Psychiatrists often treat patients with addictive behaviors that are ruining their lives.

Main Idea _____

_____

_____

4. The English paragraph has characteristics that distinguish it from paragraphs written in other languages. For one thing, the English paragraph is a separate unit of thought that has *unity*. The idea of unity requires that all of the supporting material be relevant to the main idea, unlike paragraphs in Russian or Spanish, which may contain digressions. The English paragraph also must possess *coherence*. Ideas are expressed one after another in a straight, orderly line of development. The central idea is expressed in a topic sentence. The supporting ideas are presented in a sequence that is logical to the native writer. Writers obtain the required coherence by organizing their ideas in certain acceptable ways, such as by order of importance, or spatially, or chronologically, as well as by using such transition words as *first, second, next,* etc. This straight line of development differs from a paragraph in Chinese, for example, in which thought follows a circular developmental pattern. The student learning to write an English paragraph must be aware of these rhetorical requirements that make the English paragraph different from paragraphs in many other languages. Knowing these patterns will help the student develop English proficiency.

Main Idea _____

_____

_____

You should now have a better idea of how to decide what an author's main idea is. The next step is to begin to practice outlining an author's ideas in further preparation for writing summaries.

Chapter Three
Planning for Writing

ESSAY WRITING: Planning and Organizing

Using Notes

The preceding chapters introduced the process of writing a formal essay: selecting and limiting a topic and writing effective thesis statements and introductions. The next step is to develop skills to write the body of the essay. This requires organizing your ideas. An outline is a tool to help you. It can be prepared before you write a draft of your ideas, or it can be used to organize or reorganize notes and first drafts. Remember, an outline is a tool. Like an essay, it must be revised to suit your purposes.

As you select and narrow your topic and write an effective thesis statement, you will find many ideas related to your topic. Don't let these ideas get away from you. Jot them down on a piece of paper as quickly as possible to use as supporting statements. Continue adding to your list until you have exhausted all possibilities. Don't worry about writing down too much at this point; you can always discard irrelevant ideas or less important statements later. Remember: It is easier to omit less important details after you start to write the body of your essay than it is to try to come up with new supporting material for an essay that is turning out to be too short or is not adequately developing your thesis statement.

At this point in the writing process, sit down with a partner and exchange ideas for supporting details. Often you will find that more ideas are generated when one or two other writers are brainstorming with you.

Let's look at the notes a writer might have collected for an essay with this thesis:

Several steps can be taken by individuals to help reduce present environmental problems.

Notes:

use china plates/cloth napkins

regional recycling

buy products in bulk lots

support non-polluting measures

recycle aluminum and steel ("tin") cans

use cloth diapers

recycle glass bottles/jars

recycle or reuse plastic containers

recycle newspapers/paper

sell/give away old clothes

separate recyclables from garbage

elect environmentalists to Congress

oppose companies that pollute the environment

buy environmentally safe products

support businesses that cut down on excess packaging

Go over this list. Are any of the ideas related? If so, group them together.

Preparing an Outline

In the outline below, the ideas from the list have been grouped into three categories: (I) Support environmental legislation, (II) Recycle reusable products, and (III) Support environmentally responsible businesses. This outline follows a simple traditional outline format.

> Thesis: **Several steps can be taken by individuals to reduce the present environmental problems.**

I.   Support environmental legislation.
   A.   Elect environmentalists to Congress.
   B.   Support laws/bills that promote non-polluting measures.
   C.   Support regional recycling efforts.

II.   Recycle reusable products.
   A.   Use china plates and cloth napkins.
   B.   Sell or give away old clothes.
   C.   Use cloth diapers.
   D.   Recycle newspapers and other paper products.
   E.   Recycle glass bottles and jars.
   F.   Separate recyclables from garbage.
   G.   Recycle aluminum and steel cans.
   H.   Recycle or reuse plastic containers.

III.   Support environmentally responsible businesses.
   A.   Oppose companies that pollute the environment.
   B.   Buy environmentally safe products.
   C.   Support businesses that cut down on excess packaging.
   D.   Buy products in bulk lots to reduce packaging.

> Conclusion: **By taking an active role in fighting pollution in our environment, all individuals can help to solve this world-wide problem.**

The following essay was written using the preceding outline. As you read it, notice how each paragraph is developed. Also, pay attention to the introduction. Where is the thesis statement? Does the introduction effectively catch the reader's attention? Does the essay follow the outline?

Attacking Environmental Problems

The protection of our environment is a hot topic today. Everyone talks about it, but no one seems to know what to do about the problems of cleaning up our world. People say, "I am really concerned about the environment, but I am only one person. What can one person do to make a difference?" Instead of shrugging our shoulders and silently lamenting our lost paradise, we must begin to look at the ways each person can make an impact on improving environmental conditions. Individuals can take several steps to reduce the present environmental problems.

The first step is a political one. Citizens must get involved in the governing processes that lead to protection, not destruction, of our environment. Money speaks the loudest of all; we can support right-thinking candidates with our contributions and our volunteer efforts. We can also actively support community efforts at recycling by encouraging our relatives and friends to participate in the programs.

Another way to defend our environment is to change our habits of buying and discarding products. Everyone can contribute to recycling efforts by using only products that can be reused. At the supermarket, we can pass by the paper plates, napkins, and diapers. It may take more effort on our part to wash more dishes and do more laundry, but our landfills will not become enormous trash-filled burdens on our children and their children if we stop throwing away tons of paper products. Other ways to cut down on waste include recycling newspapers and other paper publications, glass bottles and jars, aluminum and steel cans, and plastic containers. It takes a bit of planning and extra time to separate recyclables from other trash, but each individual *can* make a difference by making the effort.

Finally, individuals can make political and economic statements to the community by supporting environmentally responsible businesses. We can eat only at fast food restaurants that use recycled paper products and avoid those companies that pollute the environment. Everyone can check labels for packaging and ingredient information to avoid buying products that are not environmentally safe. Letter-writing campaigns and letters to the editors of newspapers might encourage businesses to cut down on excess packaging. We can also buy products in bulk lots to reduce the amount of packaging needed. Smart businessmen will take notice of sales volumes that increase because of their environmental responsibility or, conversely, decrease because the public refuses to support wastefulness and harm to our world.

It may be true that one drop of water will not fill an ocean; however, if we put many drops together, we can begin to make a difference. By taking an active role in fighting pollution in our environment, all individuals can help to solve this world-wide problem.

In the traditional outline, Roman numerals are used to introduce large, general topics in the body of the essay. The ideas after the Roman numerals will be found in the topic sentences of the supporting paragraphs of the body of the essay. The sentences after the letters (A,B,C) under the Roman numerals are *supporting details* of the essay. Every detail supports the idea above it in the outline. The idea of supporting details was introduced when you practiced writing paragraphs. Just as the details in A, B, and C support the topic sentences, each topic sentence supports the thesis statement.

For a more detailed outline, divide any supporting detail by using Arabic numbers (1, 2, etc.) and even further subdivide with lower case letters (a,b,c), if necessary. Remember, however, that outlining means dividing ideas into groups; this means that for every Roman numeral I, there must be a number II because you cannot divide something into fewer than two groups. Likewise, for every A, there must be a B. These are the rules for writing a formal outline.

Example:

I. Topic sentence

   A. Supporting idea

      1. detail

      2. detail

   B. Supporting idea

II. Topic sentence

   A. Supporting idea

      1. detail

      2. detail

      3. detail

   B. Supporting idea

      1. detail

         a. smaller detail

         b. smaller detail

      2. detail

Exercise 1. Organizing Notes into an Outline

With the thesis statement as a guide, use the form on the next page to organize the following notes into an outline. Find the more general and encompassing statements that should become topic sentences after Roman numerals. Which ideas should support each of these more general ideas? Which of the notes are "examples" of other ideas?

Thesis: Tennis has become a highly popular sport in the United States for several reasons.

Notes:

Many public parks have tennis courts.

Top professional players can become rich.

Tones thigh muscles.

Women can compete against men.

Equipment and playing areas are simple and widely available.

Martina Navratilova has become extremely wealthy.

Almost constant motion—a lot of muscle exercise.

Player's size not significant factor.

Increases player's strength.

Some large public high schools have indoor courts in sports centers.

Good financial prospects for players.

A small child could play with a parent.

Good exercise (uses all parts of the body).

Free indoor and outdoor courts are often available.

Professional players make fortunes from product endorsements.

A net and painted lines make up playing field.

Football player could compete with housewife.

Players are often paid to advertise tennis equipment.

Good for lungs (running increases oxygen intake).

John McEnroe became a millionaire through tennis.

Trims waist.

Racquets and balls—relatively inexpensive.

Thesis: **Tennis has become a highly popular sport in the United States for several reasons.**

(As a guide, some of this outline has been filled in.)

I. Good financial prospects for players.

    A. _____

        1. _____

        2. _____

    B. _____

        1. *Martina Navratilova has become extremely wealthy.*

        2. _____

II. _____

    A. _____

    B. _____

    C. *Trims waist.*

    D. _____

    E. _____

III. _____

    A. _____

    B. _____

    C. *Free indoor and outdoor courts are often available.*

        1. _____

        2. _____

IV. _____

    A. *A small child could play with a parent.*

    B. _____

    C. _____

Exercise 2. Revising an Outline

Sharing your ideas with your classmates can help you to organize your ideas as well as to decide on appropriate supporting material for your compositions. In this exercise, your teacher will arrange you in pairs to examine an outline for an essay on living a healthier life. With your partner, decide if anything important has been left out. Can you add supporting details to section III? Should any of the items, including the major supporting ideas, be in a different order? Can you add supporting examples or details?

Remember that an outline is just a working tool. It is not a permanent, unchangeable form. You may revise it at any time during the process of writing an essay. Write a revised form with your partner on a piece of paper.

Toward a Healthier Life

Thesis: You can lead a healthier life if you take certain steps.

(Purpose: to encourage the reader to lead a healthier life.)

I. Correct any bad habits you have.

    A. Stop smoking.

    B. Drink less alcohol.

II. Eat better.

    A. Watch fat in your diet.

    B. Include food from all food groups.

    C. Cut down on sugar.

III. Exercise regularly.

WRITING THE CONCLUSION OF THE ESSAY

The conclusion of an essay should direct the reader's attention to the essay's main points and sustain them. Imagine a mystery story in which you were not given the solution or a fairy tale that did not end with "and they all lived happily ever after." Having spent a lot of time planning and writing your essay, you certainly want a satisfying conclusion.

As with the introduction, the actual form of a conclusion depends on the type of essay. The different types of conclusions include some of the same devices suggested for introductions, such as quotations, questions, and anecdotes, but they usually refer to material that has been presented in the body of the essay. The following types are frequently used. A conclusion may also contain a combination of these types.

Result: This type of conclusion is well suited to a process/analysis essay such as the ones you will work on later in this chapter. A process essay can be concluded by giving the result or results of the process that has been described.

After you have prepared your delicious Texas-style ribs, it is now time to enjoy the wonderful dish you have prepared. Set your table attractively with a lot of napkins for messy fingers. Fill each glass with sparkling red wine, take off your apron, sit down, and begin to taste your succulent meal. You will never want to eat ribs cooked any other way. Bon appetit!

Restatement (summary): In this most common type of conclusion, the main idea is restated in different words to reinforce (for one last time) the writer's main points. In a short essay, this type of conclusion would not be appropriate, but for a long essay with an extended discussion, it is very useful.

It is clear, then, that Native Americans in the United States are still faced with significant problems. Each tribe still wants to keep its own traditions and customs. However, the young people want to enter the modern world shown to them on television and in the movies. They are anxious to have an education and a good job, but they have trouble adjusting to life in the city. In addition, Native Americans are still discriminated against. They have lost self-confidence and pride, which may be the largest challenge they must meet.

Prediction: An essay that expresses an opinion or point of view may end with a prediction. After a summary of the main points, the writer says what will happen next or in the future. In the following example, underline the prediction.

The third stage of development of the "smart" highway is still many years in the future. Although the University of California at Berkeley is presently studying a remote guidance system that will allow cars to follow a painted stripe on a highway, the ultimate system still faces many obstacles. All indications are, however, that we can look forward to a time when we will get in our cars and settle back with our paper and coffee, leaving the driving up to the highway and the car. The future may not be so far away.

Recommendation: A recommendation is most common when the writer has discussed a problem, perhaps given its causes, and now wishes to suggest a solution. In the next conclusion, the writer follows a short summary with a recommendation. Underline the recommendation.

It is obvious from what has been said that most students who study in a foreign country face some of the same difficulties, culture-shock and loneliness being the most prevalent. Therefore, I suggest that before going to a foreign country to study, each student should be required to study not only the new language but also some of the cultural differences between the native country and the new one. Most importantly, each student should be assigned a host family to help make the transition to the new lifestyle less traumatic and lonely.

Quotation: A quotation can give credence to what has been written about, especially if an authority in the field is quoted. In the example, the quotation adds authority to the author's main point.

> Thus, despite tremendous advances in computer technology, the kind of robot found in science-fiction movies is still a long way off in the future. According to MIT electronics expert Phillip Masterson, "Someday, we will be able to go into our local discount store and buy a mechanized robot that will take our commands, do our housework, and make our lives easier." Until that time, we can only dream of such mechanical humans.

In any conclusion, don't introduce an idea that you have not discussed in the body of the essay. This should not happen in a carefully planned essay, but if it does, insert the idea appropriately in the body of the essay.

Exercise 3. Writing Conclusions

Read the following essays. For each one, note the thesis statement and supporting detail. In the space provided, add an appropriate concluding paragraph. What type will you use? (This may be done as a group activity.)

How to Write an Essay
by Deborah Kresyman

Have you ever felt that it was an impossible task to write an essay? Have you ever said to a teacher, "I know what I want to say, but I just can't write it down"? Most of us feel that writing an essay is an arduous, painful task, but we can make that task much easier if we keep in mind the basic parts of an essay.

First, we need to write an introduction. This introduction is a very important part of our task because it must have the main idea or thesis of our essay in it. It should be clearly written with the help of some key words that act like tools to limit the discussion. For example, if we choose to write about food, we know that it is a vast topic, and we necessarily must limit it with key words such as *delicious, nutritious,* or *inexpensive.* Each of these key words limits our topic and helps us plan the next step of the essay.

Next, we plan and write the body of the essay. It consists of several paragraphs, each of which should include a topic sentence closely related to and supporting the thesis. For example, if the thesis statement about food contains a key word such as *nutritious,* we can develop the topic sentences for our paragraphs with ideas about vitamins, proteins, or minerals. Also, we can use several methods of paragraph development such as examples, details, contrast, or facts and statistics to support our main idea. If we are writing about nutritious food with a paragraph containing a topic sentence dealing with vitamins, we can give examples of vegetables or fruits supplying these essentials.

Finally, we must write the last part of the essay: the conclusion. Essentially, this part is a summary of the ideas in the essay. It must give the reader a clear idea of the connection between the body and the introduction, often with the purpose of the writer restated, and it should not include any new material.

Conclusion:

_____

_____

_____

_____

Choosing a College

by Lorenzo Martinez

Many factors influenced me in choosing a college at which to continue my education. From the beginning of my senior year in high school, I had been looking for the college that was right for me. Although the reputation of the college was perhaps my first consideration, I also studied other advantages. Because of its location, financial arrangements, and special programs offered, I decided to attend Maryvale Community College (MCC).

One reason I chose this college is that it is very convenient for me. Since the campus is located near my neighborhood, I can live at home while I attend classes. Although I do not have a car, taking the bus to MCC is not too inconvenient. I have to transfer once, but the trip takes only 30 minutes and there are frequent buses. Sometimes, when the weather is nice, I ride my bike to the campus. Since there are few hills between my home and the college, going by bicycle is even faster than the bus trip.

Another reason is the tuition. Tuition at MCC is lower than that of most four-year colleges, and student financial aid is available. For in-state students, the cost per semester credit is currently $50.00, which is very reasonable. Even though tuition for out-of-state students is nearly three times that amount, it is still less than tuition at private colleges. Also, as a community college, MCC was designed for students who live at home, which saves a considerable amount of room-and-board money. Furthermore, I can get a low-interest loan from the federal government to help cover my costs. There are also some scholarships and work-study programs for students who need them. In fact, by going to MCC, I will not have to worry about financial matters much at all.

Most important, however, is the fact that there are English as a Second Language classes that help foreign students improve their English communication skills. When they first arrive at the college, students who have studied little or no English in their home countries need a lot of special help in the language. The four levels of ESL courses available are especially designed for these students. The program also provides labs for listening skills and computer-assisted instruction. Because I need more work on my English, this program is a great benefit for me.

Conclusion:

Exercise 4. Writing More Conclusions

A thesis statement and supporting topic sentences are provided. In the blanks that follow each group, write an appropriate conclusion, using one of the types suggested in this chapter (result, restatement, prediction, recommendation, or quotation).

A. Thesis: **Attending college is much more difficult than attending high school.**

1. Once we attend college, many of us are working, often full-time.
2. The course requirements are much more demanding.
3. We are responsible for choosing our courses and making sure we meet the graduation requirements.
4. We are forced to make difficult career decisions at this point in our lives if we have not done so already.

Conclusion:

B. Thesis: The computer age is affecting our lives in more ways than we ever imagined.

1. It is affecting us in the area of entertainment.
2. It is affecting us in the area of business.
3. It is affecting us in the area of education.
   Conclusion:

   _____

   _____

   _____

   _____

C. Thesis: Walking has become very popular in the United States for several reasons.

1. It is relatively inexpensive, requiring very little equipment.
2. It is excellent for the health, especially for the cardiovascular system.
3. It is good for the morale of the participant.
   Conclusion:

   _____

   _____

   _____

   _____

D. Thesis: A library is much more than a place to check out books to read for entertainment.

1. It offers audio-visual material: films, records, and tapes.
2. It provides much public-information material, including college catalogs, employment listings, and minutes of public meetings of concern to the citizen.
3. It offers story hours, movies, crafts, concerts, and summer and holiday programs for children.
4. It offers research materials and expert aid by professional librarians for the serious academic.
   Conclusion:

   _____

   _____

   _____

   _____

Exercise 5. Collaborative Planning of an Essay

Work with the same partner who helped you in Exercise 2. Using your revised outline from Exercise 2, you and your partner will now collaborate on a first draft of a composition. One of you will write an introduction and a conclusion, and the other will write the body. Review the different types of introductions suggested in Chapter Two for some ideas. Also, decide together how you want to end the essay. Perhaps you would like to give a recommendation on beginning a program to lead a healthier life.

The partner who writes the body is to use the outline as a guide. This person can change the details in the outline if necessary, but both of you together should decide on any changes that might affect the thesis statement or the conclusion.

Writing About a Process

Giving instructions may be as simple as telling someone how to get from one place to another or showing someone how to cook a delicious dish from your native country. On the other hand, you may be asked to explain a more complex process. Your history teacher may ask you to explain how ancient farmers prepared their fields, or your biology teacher may want you to show how blood flows through the body. In giving directions, the reader may actually perform the process; in contrast, when you explain some processes, you do not expect the reader to try to carry them out. Both types of essays, however, involve describing a process completely and in orderly steps.

Several hints can help you write a good process essay.

First, consider your audience. How well acquainted is your reader with the topic? How detailed must you be? How much can you take for granted? Is there special vocabulary that you must explain? For example, you may have changed the oil in your car dozens of times, but if your mother has decided to try her hand at this process, you had better include every necessary step in the process when you explain to her how to do it.

Second, include all of the steps of the process in the correct order. Nothing is more exasperating than being told the steps in a process out of order. Imagine reading a recipe that told you to add three eggs to your mixture. After doing this, imagine that the recipe later says to separate the yolks from the whites and beat the egg whites before adding them. You would have to throw out all of your ingredients and start over.

Next, remember to give the final step in the process. Do not take it for granted that the reader will infer the correct final step. An anecdote may help emphasize the importance of this: A government worker once called her husband, who was already at home, to tell him that she was leaving her office and to ask him to put a casserole into a preheated oven. Her subway car subsequently broke down on the way home, delaying her in an underground tunnel for over two hours. The moment she walked into her apartment, she smelled the strong odor of burning food. Hurrying to the kitchen, she found her casserole still in the hot oven and the food burned beyond recognition. "Why didn't you turn off the oven?" she asked her husband. "You never told me to turn it *off*," was his reply. Don't let this happen to you! Be clear in giving the important last step.

Finally, use appropriate verb forms. When you write instructions, you usually write in the imperative: "First, *get out* the ingredients; then, *cut* the carrots into small pieces; next, *put* them into a saucepan." Sometimes instructions are written in the present tense, using the subject *you*: "First, *you get out* the ingredients," etc; or modal verbs are used: "Then, *you must cut* the carrots into small pieces." In essays that explain a process, the third person active or passive verb is used: "Ancient farmers first cleared fields of trees or shrubs before planting; fields were marked before seeds were planted." Remember that whatever verb form you select should be appropriate to the type of essay and used consistently throughout.

Transitions

Transition words that indicate the movement from one step to another are used in process/analysis essays. The following words and phrases are often used.

The	first second next last final	step phase stage	(is...)

Then, *Next,* *Afterwards,* *After this step,* *Finally,*	heat the pan over a medium flame. break an egg into a bowl. scramble the egg with a fork. add salt and pepper to the eggs. fry the eggs, turning them frequently.

Exercise 6. Using Process Transition Words

Put the steps in the following directions in an appropriate order. Then write a paragraph on this process, adding transition words.

Making a Pot of Coffee

a. Turn off the coffee maker.

b. Measure the water and put it into the coffee maker.

c. Decide how many cups of coffee you want to make.

d. Measure coffee into the filter. (1 measure for every 2 cups of coffee. Adjust amounts for stronger or weaker coffee.)

e. Wait until all the water has run through the coffee.

f. Take out a paper coffee filter and place it in the filter holder of the coffee maker.

g. Serve the coffee with cream and sugar, as desired.

h. Turn on the coffee maker.

i. Put the filter holder into the coffee maker.

Use this topic sentence to begin your paragraph:

Making a pot of delicious coffee is a very simple process if you follow these directions.

Exercise 7. Following Directions

Do this exercise with the whole class. Draw the design described below. Don't peek at the answer at the bottom of the page!

1. Put your pencil at a point one inch above the center of the bottom of a piece of paper. Label this "point A." Draw a two-inch vertical line up from point A. Label the point at the top "point B."

2. Put your pencil at a point one-half inch down from point B. Label this "point C." Draw a one-inch line to the left of point C and perpendicular to line AB. Label the end of this line "point D." Draw another one-inch line to the right of point C and perpendicular to line AB. Label the end of this line "point E."

3. Draw a straight line from point B to point D. Draw another straight line from point B to point E.

4. Put your pencil at point A, and draw a one-fourth-inch wide U to the left of point A. What do you have? Were the directions well-written?

Exercise 8. Writing and Following Directions

Your teacher will divide the class into groups of three or four. Each group is to write directions like those in Exercise 7 on how to draw a

(Answer: an open umbrella)

simple design. Then groups will exchange directions and try to draw the designs.

Have someone in your group draw a simple design such as a stick figure or the outline of some object. (HINT: The best artist in the group may not be the most appropriate person to draw the figure. Good artists tend to want to draw very complicated or detailed figures. Remember, your group will have to describe the process of drawing the figure.)

Everyone in the group should help decide what to draw and how to draw it. Choose one person to serve as recorder to write down the directions for drawing the figure on a *separate* piece of paper (not the same one on which you draw the design). Write down the directions as a list, being sure to include all the essential steps in the appropriate order. You may not use descriptive nouns in your list. (For example, if you draw a face, you cannot say "Draw a face." You must say, "Draw a circle...etc.") After you finish, check over the directions carefully to make sure they are clear.

Next, exchange your directions only (not the drawing) with another group that will try to duplicate the original drawing from the directions given to you. The group that writes the best directions will be the one whose design is duplicated best by another group. (That group will be the "winners" in following directions.)

STRUCTURE REVIEW: Participial Phrases

The underlined verbs in the following paragraph are *participles, -ing and -ed (or equivalent) forms of verbs used as modifiers.* In the following paragraph, all of the participles modify nouns, thus functioning as adjectives. The whole participial phrase is in bold print.

Since the turn of the century, men had tried to run a mile in less than 4 minutes, but it wasn't until 1954 that Roger Bannister, <u>dedicated</u> **to attaining that goal,** was able to do so. Bannister, <u>being</u> **a medical student,** used his medical knowledge to slow his pulse rate so that his heart received a greater amount of oxygen with each beat. Thus, because his pulse rate increased while he was running, he had a greater oxygen supply. Chris Basher ran with Bannister to set the pace. <u>Having set</u> **too fast a pace,** Basher fell down <u>exhausted</u> half way. Three hundred yards from the finish, Bannister, <u>cheered</u> **by the crowds,** began to kick higher and lengthen his stride. Then, <u>crossing</u> **the finish line,** he fell painfully to the ground, almost unconscious. Bannister had run the race in 3 minutes, 59.4 seconds, a new record. He had broken the 4-minute mile!

Participles can also be used single to modify nouns, as in the following sentences:

This is a very *boring* lecture.

The *bored* students are starting to leave.

When the modified noun *causes* the reaction, the participle is in the present (*-ing*) form. When the noun *receives* or *feels the effects of* the action, the participle is in the past form (*-ed* or equivalent for irregular verbs). Another way to think of this is that when the participle comes from a verb in the *active* form, it is the *-ing* form. When it comes from the *passive* form, it is the *-ed* (or equivalent) form.

Doer/causer = verb + *ing*   Done to/receiver = verb + *ed*
(Active)   (Passive)

Exercise 1. Choosing Single-Participial Modifiers

Choose the correct present or past participial form. The first exercise has been done for you.

1. The exhibit *fascinated* the tourists.

   The exhibit was *fascinating*_____.

   The tourists were *fascinated*_____.

2. The story *amused* the children.

   The children were _____.

   The story was _____.

3. The gift *surprised* the boss.

   The boss was _____.

   The gift was _____.

4. The comment *insulted* the teacher.

   The teacher was _____.

   The comment was _____.

5. His school records *amazed* the admissions officer.

   His school records were _____.

   The admissions officer was _____.

Exercise 2. Forming Single-Participial Modifiers

Choose the *-ing* or *-ed* participle form of the verb in parentheses to use in the blank. The first has been done for you.

1. The student was _____ *elated* _____ (elate) when he received the news of his acceptance to Harvard.

2. The teacher said, "I am _____ (please) to announce that the test results were good."

3. The mystery writer is one of the best _____ (know) authors in the U.S. today. (Note: "know" has an irregular past partiple.)

4. The president reported that he had had a very _____ (satisfy) meeting with the other world leaders.

5. Sometimes _____ (flatter) remarks do more harm than good.

6. Being _____ (depress) by the death of her close friend, Sue took a few days off from work.

7. She was happy to hear the _____ (reassure) words of her boss, especially since she had made such a bad mistake.

8. John is such an _____ (amuse) person that everyone likes to invite him to parties.

9. We are _____ (interest) in buying a house, but the interest rates are just too high.

10. There is _____ (overwhelm) evidence that there is a direct link between smoking and cancer.

11. The directions that we were given were so _____ (mislead) that we never made it to the party.

The *present participle*, also called the active participle, usually takes place at the same time as the action of the main verb:

> *Listening to the radio,* Barbara hummed to the music while doing her housework. (The action of the participle takes place at the same times as the action of the main verb.)

Using adverbial expressions can change the time relationship between the participle and the main verb:

> *After eating* supper, Juan went out to play baseball.
>
> *Before doing* his homework, Adam always has a little snack.
>
> *Upon hearing* about the tornado warnings, everyone hurried home. (*Upon* = immediately after)

Exercise 3. Using Present and Past Participles

Complete each sentence with a present or past participial phrase. Use the suggested verb. The first has been done for you.

1. The workmen (work) _____*working on the bridge repair*_____ receive overtime pay on Saturday.

2. All students (receive) _____ will be honored at a special assembly next week.

3. The children (sell) _____ are trying to raise money for new band uniforms.

4. The new computers (locate) _____ were bought at great expense.

5. The actor (appear) _____ is well known around the world.

6. The statue (carve) _____ is a wonderful example of religious art of the sixteenth century.

7. Students (attend) _____ often have trouble adjusting to a new system of teaching.

8. Apartment houses (locate) _____ are very desirable.

9. Schools (offer) _____ are very popular.

10. Before (take) _____, the student studied for days.

11. After (leave) _____, Mary realized that she had left her purse there.

12. Mother always told us to hang up our jackets upon (arrive) _____ each afternoon.

Passive progressive participles (*being* + verb + *ed* or equivalent) can be used for *present* or *future* time.

Examples: The class *being held* now in that classroom is a German course.

The lecture *being given* tomorrow will be very interesting.

Perfect participles (active: *having* + verb + *ed* or equivalent; passive: *having* + *been* + verb + *ed* or equivalent) show that the action of the participial phrase occurred *before* the action of the main verb.

Examples: Roger Bannister, *having dedicated* himself to attaining his goal, was able to break the 4-minute mile.

Chris Basher, *having set* too fast a pace, fell down exhausted.

This house, *having been rented* for over ten years, needs a paint job badly.

The *perfect participle* often appears at the beginning of the sentence, before the subject it modifies. Place the word *not* before a progressive or perfect participle to make the phrase negative.

> Example: *Not having finished high school*, the job applicant was not considered for the position.

Exercise 4. Completing Sentences with Progressive and Perfect Participles

A participial phrase is given. Complete each sentence. The first has been done for you.

1. Having returned from his trip abroad, the president *held a peace confer-ence at the White House*   .

2. Having applied for a passport, ——————————————————
——————————————————————————————.

3. The nurses, having worked all night, ——————————————
——————————————————————————————.

4. The baby, having slept all afternoon, ——————————————
——————————————————————————————.

5. Having eaten already, ——————————————————————
——————————————————————————————.

6. The tourists, having seen all the sights, —————————————
——————————————————————————————.

7. The students, having spent the whole day in the library, ——————
——————————————————————————————.

8. Not having passed the entrance exam, —————————————
——————————————————————————————.

Reducing Adverbial Clauses to Participial Phrases

Adverbial clauses expressing *time* and *cause* relationships may be reduced to adverbial phrases using participles. This adds variety to the sentence structure of essays, making the writing more interesting. The type of participle used to reduce adverbial clauses depends on the sequence of the events (actions or states) in the adverbial and main clauses. Observe how they are used in the following examples. Also, notice that the subjects of both clauses must be identical, and the subject is named in the independent clauses.

Use the *present participle* (active or passive) when the events of the two clauses are simultaneous (occurring at the same time) or when a *causal* relationship is expressed.

Examples:

While the spectators watched the soccer match, they cheered for their favorite.
*While **watching** the soccer match,* the spectators cheered for their favorite.

Because John needed cash, he went to an automatic teller machine.
***Needing** cash,* John went to an automatic teller machine.

When the painting is seen from up close, it appears to be only masses of dots.
***Seen** from up close,* the painting appears to be only masses of dots.

Also use the *present participle* (active or passive) when an adverbial conjunction (*before* or *after*) makes the time relationship clear.

Examples:

After the soldiers lowered the flag, they marched away.
*After **lowering** the flag,* the soldiers marched away.

Before Margaret bought a new car, she shopped around at several dealers.
*Before **buying** a new car,* Margaret shopped around at several dealers.

Use the *perfect participle* (active or passive) when the event of the adverbial clause precedes the event of the main clause. Causal actions occurring before the main clause also use the perfect participle. The adverbial conjunction *after* is unnecessary when the perfect participle is used.

Examples:

After Juan had made a home run in the baseball game, he celebrated with his teammates.
***Having made** a home run in the baseball game,* Juan celebrated with his teammates.

After Ryan was given an award for his fine art work, he was recognized by all the students at his school.
***Having been given** an award for his fine art work,* Ryan was recognized by all the students at his school.

Because Patrick had found a valuable coin, he was able to make enough money from its sale to buy a new bike.
***Having found** a valuable coin,* Patrick was able to make enough money from its sale to buy a new bike.

Exercise 5. Reducing Adverbial Clauses to Participial Phrases

Following the examples, change the adverbial clause in each sentence to a participial phrase. There may be more than one possible answer. The first is done for you.

1. After Shana and Rachel met in the third grade, they became very close friends.

   After meeting in the third grade, Shana and Rachel became very close friends.

2. When they swam together during vacation, they always liked to race against each other.

   _____

   _____

3. After they had practiced swimming and diving for several years, they had become quite good.

   _____

   _____

4. When Rachel was chosen for her club's diving team, she was very excited. (Change "she" to "Rachel" when you rewrite.)

   _____

   _____

5. After she had competed in several diving events, she became known as one of the best young divers in the state.

   _____

   _____

6. Meanwhile, when Shana was observed by the coach of the State Swimming Association, she was selected to swim for that team. (Change "she" to "Shana" when you rewrite.)

   _____

   _____

7. After she had swum against the best freestyle competitors of her age group, she became the regional champion.

   _____

   _____

8. While Rachel and Shana worked to perfect their styles, they often thought about the Olympic Games. (Change "they" to "Rachel and Shana" when you rewrite.)

   _____

   _____

9. Because they had become champions in their sports, they decided to try out for the U.S. Olympic team.

   _____

   _____

10. While they trained for the Olympic trials, they became even closer friends, always helping and encouraging each other.

    _____

    _____

11. When they had finally been chosen for the Olympic team, they were both exuberant.

    _____

    _____

12. While they traveled to the site of the Olympic games, Shana and Rachel vowed to cheer each other on to gold medals.

    _____

    _____

Reducing Adjective Clauses to Participial Phrases

Adjective clauses may also be reduced to participial phrases to add more variety to writing. The rules for reducing adjective clauses are simple:

1. Adjective clauses containing *who, which,* or *that* as subjects of the clause may be reduced.
2. If you have a form of the verb *to be,* omit the relative pronoun (*who, which* or *that*) and omit the form of the verb *to be:*

   > Students *who are planning* to graduate this year must notify the dean.
   > Students *planning* to graduate this year must notify the dean.

   > Some teachers like to receive papers *that are written* in ink.
   > Some teachers like to receive papers *written* in ink.

3. Some verbs that do not contain a form of the verb *to be* may also be reduced. Omit the relative pronoun and change the verb to the present (*-ing*) participle.

   > Students *who plan* to graduate this year must notify the dean.
   > Students *planning* to graduate this year must notify the dean.

Participial phrases that modify the subject of the main clause and that are formed from reducing non-essential adjective clauses (those set off from the rest of the sentence with commas) often precede the sentence.

This house, *which has not been painted* for many years, will not withstand the cold weather this winter.

Not having been painted for many years, this house will not withstand the cold weather this winter.

The foreign students, *who had registered early*, were able to get the classes they needed.

Having registered early, the foreign students were able to get the classes they needed.

Exercise 6. Reducing Adjective Clauses to Participial Phrases

Following the examples, change the adjective clauses to participial phrases. The first is done for you.

1. Of the many holy books that are used by people of the world today, the Koran, the Bible, and the Bhagavad-Gita are the oldest and best known.

    Of the many holy books used by people of the world today, the Koran, the Bible and the Bhagavad-Gita are the oldest and best known.

2. The Koran, which was probably first started in 633 A.D., contains the word of God recited by the prophet Mohammed.

    _____

    _____

3. The Koran, which consists of 77,934 words, is arranged in 114 chapters.

    _____

    _____

4. The Bible, which contains both the Old and the New Testaments, is the holy book of Christianity.

    _____

    _____

5. The Old Testament is a set of laws, history, and literary writings that were originally found on scrolls and were believed to date back to around the twelfth century B.C.

    _____

    _____

6. The Bible, which had been written many years before Mohammed's birth, was probably familiar to him. (Begin the sentence with the participial phrase.)

    _____

    _____

7. Many of the stories that appear in the Koran make reference to stories and people in the Bible.

    _____

    _____

8. The Bhagavad-Gita is part of a longer work, the Mahabharata, which is thought to be the longest poem in the world, with over one million verses.

    _____

    _____

Exercise 7. Using Participles in Paragraphs

Write the appropriate participial form of the verbs in parentheses. Both active and passive participles will be used.

Taking medicine carelessly can be a very unpleasant and even dangerous experience. A few weeks ago, I started to suffer from all the symptoms of a cold. _____ (Feel) that dry, harsh sensation in the throat and _____ (have) watery eyes and a runny nose, I looked for some cold pills in my medicine cabinet and found a bottle of cold tablets. _____ (Give) to me by a friend, these pills were not supposed to cause drowsiness; on the contrary, _____ (compare) to most cold medicine, this medicine is a bit of a stimulant. I took two tablets right before _____ (go) to bed.

After _____ (sleep) very restlessly, I finally got up at dawn, _____ (curse) the cold for all the discomfort I was experiencing. At breakfast, I took another dosage of those little red pills. Throughout the day, _____ (go) about my regular activities, I was feeling uncomfortable and irritable. Every two hours, faithfully, I took the medicine, but by the end of the afternoon, my cold symptoms were no better, and I was feeling awful.

Around 6:00 p.m., _____ (take) eight pills so far that day, I walked to my girlfriend's house for dinner. Even though she lived only a few blocks away, I arrived _____ (feel) as if I had walked for miles. _____ (make) the arrangements several days before, I could not cancel the dinner date because I knew my girlfriend had spent hours preparing a nice meal. I managed to make it to her house and practically collapsed on her sofa. _____ (Question) by my girlfriend about my weak appearance, I explained about my cold. The person who had given me the pills happened to be at the dinner party. He told me that the dosage of the medicine was the problem. An adult should take only one tablet every six hours, not _____ (exceed) four tablets in twenty-four hours! No wonder I felt so terrible! In twelve hours, _____ (take) eight of those little red things, I had already exceeded the maximum dosage by double! For that reason, I had been awake for nearly two days in a row!

Being very careful about medicine is really important, as I learned. Never again will I take medicine I am not familiar with before _____ (read) the directions and warnings on the label. Otherwise, I might find myself feeling much worse than before _____ (take) the drug in the first place!

From an essay by Marcio Pancera, student

Exercise 8. Sentence Combining

Review the sections on participial phrases in this chapter before doing this exercise. Join each pair of numbered sentences, using participles when appropriate. Do not change unnumbered sentences. You may add adverbs and change the order of the pairs of sentences. Write in paragraph form.

Once upon a time, there was a beautiful little girl named Lauren. Lauren's parents had left her at an orphanage when she was very small because they were too poor to care for her. One day, the orphanage was forced to close, so all of the children were moved to an orphanage in another city. Her parents did not know where she was, and Lauren was forced to work very hard by the cruel director, Ms. Cratchit. *(1)* First, she scrubbed the floors every morning. *(1)* Then she took out the trash. While the other children napped, Lauren had to do her school work. *(2)* She was forced to serve meals to the other children. *(2)* Then she was fed leftovers in the kitchen. *(3)* She finished her chores late at night. *(3)* Then she fell into bed, exhausted. Lauren always felt very sad, but she was sweet-tempered, so she never complained.

One day, a handsome couple visited the orphanage. *(4)* The woman was dressed in an expensive suit. *(4)* She looked very prosperous. *(5)* The gentleman showed his identification to the attendant. *(5)* He asked to see the head of the orphanage. *(6)* The couple was taken to Ms. Cratchit's office. *(6)* Then they explained who they were. They were little Lauren's parents, and they had reversed their fortunes by working very hard over the years. *(7)* They had been searching for Lauren for over a year. *(7)* Now they wished to reclaim their darling daughter.

(8) Ms. Cratchit was very impressed with the parents' story and with their obvious wealth. *(8)* She assured the couple that Lauren had been well cared for over the years. *(9)* Ms. Cratchit sent for Lauren, who appeared at the office in a dirty dress. *(9)* She looked very thin and tired. *(10)* The parents hugged their child. *(10)* They explained who they were. *(11)* Lauren had dreamed often of this moment. *(11)* She could hardly believe it was true. *(12)* The parents took their little girl home with them immediately. *(12)* They angrily denounced the director for her mistreatment of their daughter. Little Lauren lived happily ever after with her family, and the parents made sure that no child at that orphanage was ever again treated cruelly.

WRITING ASSIGNMENT ONE:

Writing Directions Together

Your teacher will divide the class into groups for writing. You and the others in your group are to write an essay on the topic: "How to obtain a driver's license in this state." As you prepare for writing, imagine that you are writing this for someone who has recently arrived in the United States, so you must give a lot of detail.

1. Make a group list of all the steps required to obtain a driver's license in your state. Include as many details as you can. (HINT: Did you start at the very beginning of the process...getting information from the license bureau about the process? Did you discuss studying for the written exam? Practicing your driving skill for the behind-the-wheel test?)

2. Look over the list and see if you can find any broad, general categories of ideas. Begin to group related ideas.

3. Write an outline of your ideas. Put ideas from your list into the outline. Add details wherever you can.

4. Decide how to divide the writing of the essay. Different group members need to write the introduction, parts of the body, and the conclusion.

5. Write the essay. The group members who wrote the various parts of the outline should write the corresponding sections of the first draft.

6. Exchange your section of the essay with another group member. Read your partner's part for the purpose of revising and editing. Did he or she omit any steps in the process? Will someone who is attempting to get a driver's license find the directions useful? Revise your section, taking account of your partner's comments.

7. Assign one group member to assemble the essay draft. (See Appendix 3 for computer directions.) This person should add connectors for unity and cohesion where appropriate.

8. Edit the draft for grammar, spelling, and punctuation errors. Each group member should have a chance to see and approve the final version before turning it in to your teacher.

WRITING ASSIGNMENT TWO:

Writing Directions on Your Own

Choose one of the *Giving Directions* or *Describing a Process* topics and develop an essay on that topic. Follow the same kind of process of revising that you used with your group in Writing Assignment One. Before you turn your first draft in to your teacher, be sure to edit it for grammar, spelling, and punctuation errors.

GIVING DIRECTIONS
1. How to take a good photograph.
2. How to live on a budget.
3. How to vote intelligently.
4. How to apply for a loan.
5. How to buy a good used car.
6. How to diet successfully.
7. How to run a scientific experiment.
8. *Your choice:* Write about an unusual process that you know how to perform. Perhaps you have a hobby, such as training a pet, that involves a process you can share with the reader.

DESCRIBING A PROCESS
1. How people in your country celebrate a holiday.

2. How farms are run in your country.
3. How photosynthesis works.
4. How population can be controlled.
5. How stars die.
6. How computers process information.
7. How an automobile engine works.
8. *Your choice:* Describe a process you know about. You can use something you have learned in one of your high school or college courses.

SUMMARY WRITING
Part Three: Outlining for Summary Writing

Outlining is used by many writers to organize their ideas before they begin to write. It is also used in other ways, one of which is to analyze what another author has written. The same kind of outlining that you did in preparation for writing is a useful step in writing summaries because it is a way of putting down the main ideas of the author in a visual form. In this lesson, you will practice outlining texts.

Exercise. Restating Main Ideas: Outlining

Prepare an outline for each essay. First, find the thesis statement, and then underline each main supporting idea. Restate the ideas to complete the outline form.

Exercise

by Patrick Henry Johns

Exercise has become an important fact of life for most people in the United States. With so many people now working in jobs with little physical movement involved, more and more people are turning to exercise for the physical conditioning that their bodies need. Before beginning an exercise program, however, people should take some preliminary steps.

I.   First, individuals need to determine whether they should exercise or not. This is especially true for people over thirty-five and smokers. Also, young adults who have been inactive should proceed slowly. Would-be exercisers should go to a physician for a physical evaluation that includes an exercise-stress test that monitors blood pressure, pulse rate, oxygen consumption, and the heart's electrical activity. Such a test can detect cardiovascular problems.

II.   Next, exercisers need to develop an exercise program based on the amount of exercise needed to condition the body without strain. This involves finding the target zone, or safe-training pulse rate, by subtracting the age from 220 and then taking a percent of that total. Beginning exercisers should use 60%, while those already in good condition can use 80%. They then take their pulse rate while exercising. If the pulse rate is above the determined percent, there might be too much strain on the body and the exercise should be changed.

III. Whatever exercise program is selected, warm-up periods before exercise are important. These should include stretching exercises and perhaps some walking. Warm-up is important to avoid the sudden strain put on the body or the muscles once exercise begins.

Improving and maintaining physical condition is without a doubt something that should concern everyone. However, jumping into an exercise routine with no planning can be more dangerous than no exercise at all. Carrying out the preliminary steps before embarking on an exercise program can help a person feel healthier, look better, and even live longer.

Thesis statement: _____

_____

I. (Main supporting idea) _____

_____

II. (Main supporting idea) _____

_____

III. (Main supporting idea) _____

_____

How an Acupuncture Doctor Works

by Dr. Vinh Truong

If you've ever had a headache and aspirin didn't help, or if you've been to the doctor and he can never find out why it hurts, perhaps you need acupuncture. Doctors using this traditional Chinese medical method can often bring about a cure when other methods are ineffective. However, before going to an acupuncturist, you should know the steps used in healing a patient.

I.   First of all, the doctor talks to the patient to encourage him and give him confidence to conquer the disease. The doctor tells him how to deal with some phenomena that might appear during the treatment process. For instance, the patient is told to relax his muscles when he is being punctured with the metal needles that are part of the treatment. After the needle goes to a certain depth in the body, the patient might have some normal numbness, so the doctor should tell the patient to express his feelings in time in order to assist in the treatment. After this explanation, the patient will be psychologically prepared for the treatment.

II.   Next, the doctor carefully examines the patient and determines the method of treatment she will use. Whether needles are to be applied first and then moxibustion, a heat application, or whether both will be applied simultaneously depends upon the patient's condition. After determining which method to use, the doctor chooses the acupuncture points for treatment.

III.   Third, the doctor selects needles of a length corresponding to the body build of the patient and decides on the location of the acupuncture points. After sterilizing the skin on and around the points with an alcohol solution, the doctor inserts and manipulates the needles at the chosen points in order to stimulate the function of the body and to cure the illness. In addition, if the patient needs moxibustion, the doctor ignites a stick and applies it above the selected point from a distance of about three centimeters, where she keeps the stick until the local area becomes pink, generally in five to ten minutes.

IV.   Finally, the doctor tells the patient about postoperative procedure. For example, the patient must rest for ten minutes after the treatment and must wait for a specified period of time before bathing. The doctor also emphasizes the importance of returning for a follow-up consultation at the proper time since most patients require more than one acupuncture treatment.

Most acupuncture doctors follow these same steps; you can use them as a rough guide in determining whether an acupuncturist you consult can be trusted. Although acupuncture may seem to be a strange kind of medical treatment, it has been used effectively for centuries in China. If that bad back doesn't improve, give acupuncture a try!

Thesis statement: _____

_____

I. (Main supporting idea) _____

_____

II. (Main supporting idea) _____

_____

III. (Main supporting idea) _____

_____

IV. (Main supporting idea) _____

_____

Chapter Four
Focus on Content

ESSAY WRITING: Classifying and Comparing

In everyday living, we all have to use logic in order to cope with our world. We try to impose order on the things, ideas, and objects around us. Let's think about something as simple as doing laundry.

When we do laundry, we often separate our clothes into logical piles before we put them in the wash. We separate the light-colored clothing from the dark. In the process, we probably have all of our dirty clothes in a basket or in a pile on the floor. We then pick out the white (or light) clothes and put them in one pile and separate the dark clothes into another pile. In the "light" pile, we may have our underwear, socks, and white shirts and blouses. In the "dark" pile, we may have our dark socks, dark shirts and blouses, and jeans. So within each pile we have a variety of types of clothing. We have looked at the whole pile and divided it according to our system of "dark" and "light."

Suppose that we then go to our bedroom and find that we have more dirty clothes to wash. We look at these new pieces to see which pile we will put them in, according to the system we have already established.

In the first case, we looked at the whole (the original pile) to see how we could divide it. In the second case, we looked at individual items (from our bedroom) and decided into which of the established categories (piles) they would go.

In writing, we call the process of systematically separating items *classification.* A writer goes through much the same process. After finding a topic, a writer gathers the material to write about (like the basket of laundry), analyzes it, and decides on logical parts (like the light and dark clothes) to present it to the reader in the most effective way. If more ideas come to the writer later (like the dirty clothes we found in the bedroom), he or she will decide which of the established categories they fit into. This organization of the material helps the writer organize thoughts. It also helps the reader follow the writer's thought more easily.

Dividing and Classifying Ideas

Exercise 1. Finding Principles of Classification and Categories

Suppose you want to describe your class. What are some things you could write about? The course content? The types of homework? The students?

Let's look at the students. Remember that when we talked about separating the laundry, we divided it into "light" and "dark," but we could have divided it into some other categories such as "delicates" and "wash and wear." What are some of the categories (logical parts) you could divide students into? What are the principles of classification? One example is given to you. Can you think of others?

Principle of Classification	Categories (Logical Parts)	Students
1. Native language	Spanish	Maria, Juan, Jose
	Arabic	Amir, Mohammad
	Vietnamese	Tuan, Lin, Chou
2. _____	_____	_____
	_____	_____
	_____	_____
3. _____	_____	_____
	_____	_____
	_____	_____

(You may add as many classification principles and categories as you can think of.)

Exercise 2. Completing Categories

Look at the following list, in which a topic and principle of classification are given. With a group of classmates, fill in the categories (logical parts) for that classification. In the first two, one category is given.

Topic	Principle of Classification	Categories (Logical Parts)
Teachers	According to how they grade	Easy _____ _____ _____
Music	According to types	Classical _____ _____ _____
Government	According to types	_____ _____ _____
Insurance	According to types	_____ _____ _____

Exercise 3. Determining Classification

In the last exercise, you were given the principle of classification, and you had to determine the categories. In this exercise, the categories are given. What are the principles of classification?

Topic	Principle of Classification	Categories (Logical Parts)
Soldiers	_____	Generals Captains Lieutenants Sergeants

Language	_____	Listening
		Speaking
		Reading
		Writing
Jobs	_____	Professionals
		Blue-collar workers
		Skilled laborers
		Unskilled
Jobs	_____	Graduate degree
		College degree
		Technical training
		High School diploma

Exercise 4. Finding Categories in Introductions

As we saw in Chapter Two, the logical parts of an essay are often made clear by the writer in the introduction. Read the following introductions to essays and underline the words or phrases that suggest the principle of classification and the categories into which the author has divided the topic.

1. In my country, men and women have well-defined, time-honored roles and positions in the society. Women are expected to demonstrate the qualities of obedience, modesty, and generosity. Men look for such qualities in prospective brides because these virtues equip women for the roles they are expected to play in the family. Girls are taught at a very early age that displaying these characteristics will make them attractive to well-intentioned suitors.

2. Over 200 years ago, the founders of the American republic gathered to write the constitution that would govern the new nation. These men were concerned about three basic rights that had been stated in the Declaration of Independence: the rights to life, liberty, and the pursuit of happiness. In a document that has withstood the test of two centuries, the writers of the U.S. Constitution ensured the American citizen of various applications of the three rights. Even today, Americans battle with words to preserve the ideas brought forth by the first U.S. citizens many years ago.

3. Many experts say that children shouldn't be allowed to watch TV because it has bad effects and is a waste of time. However, some programs are educational and worthwhile for youngsters. For example, there are nature programs, after school specials, and programs such as "Sesame Street" that help children learn to read. I believe children should be encouraged to watch these educational programs because they may learn about many things that are outside of their limited everyday experiences.

4. The hot steam rose from the asphalt like a cloud as I drove down the highway on my way to Salvador. Lush gardens surrounded the low, white-washed farm buildings that dotted the sugarcane fields. Barefoot women with near-naked toddlers scurrying close by entered houses where doors and windows were closed only against occasional showers. It was on this trip to Brazil that I observed how greatly climate has influenced the country's economy, architecture, and people.

5. Gasoline prices keep creeping upward, the roads are becoming more crowded, and the air is getting more polluted. Because of these increasing hazards, people are being urged more and more to use mass forms of transit rather than move about in personal automobiles. Using mass transit has several advantages that make it the most recommended means of transportation. It saves money, time, and energy. Shouldn't we consider these advantages before pulling the family car out of the garage?

In an essay, the writer is expected to present ideas logically. Next, we will look at the logic used when ideas are compared and/or contrasted.

Comparing and Contrasting Ideas

Comparing is showing similarities between persons, objects, and ideas; *contrasting* is showing differences. Comparing and contrasting are ways to show relationships. Most of us compare and contrast in some form every day. We may comparison shop, for example. Also, mothers explaining things to children often rely on comparison and contrast, as do language teachers:

A cup is like a glass except that it has a handle.

A billboard and a bulletin board are both places to display advertisements or notices, but a billboard is found outdoors along the highway, and a bulletin board is found in the home, school, or office.

There is usually no comparison without some contrast, since there would be no need to compare two identical items. Likewise, we are unlikely to express contrast without some comparison, since there would be no purpose in contrasting two items that did not have some element in common.

Comparison and contrast is used as a means of presenting ideas on a variety of topics. It is used frequently by history professors discussing different periods of time in history, by anthropologists describing different cultures, by sociologists comparing different social groups, and by philosophers contrasting theories. It is especially useful for those writers who try to make difficult scientific and technical topics more understandable for the lay person, and it is commonly used in persuasive speaking or writing, when the writer is trying to convince the reader of the advantages of one point of view compared to another.*

Comparison and contrast is not an end in itself, but writers compare and contrast as a way to support and develop their ideas. Two basic organization patterns, or a combination of them, are used, and the one an author uses depends on the topic and audience.

Item-by-item: One method is *item-by-item* comparison, in which one item or idea is totally described and then the other is similarly described. Here is an example of an outline using item-by-item organization to compare two colleges, Hammond College and Williamsburg College.

Notice the form of the outline. Roman numerals are used to mark the two large divisions of the topic (Hammond College, Williamsburg College). Capital letters mark the points that will be discussed about each college. Notice that the same order of ideas under A, B, and C is used in both section I and II.

Thesis: **Although both Hammond College and Williamsburg College share similarities as "community colleges," they are different in several ways.**

I. Hammond College
   A. Student population
   B. Special services
   C. Recent enrollment patterns

II. Williamsburg College
   A. Student population
   B. Special services
   C. Recent enrollment patterns

Using this two-part pattern, all the information about Hammond College and then all the information about Williamsburg College is presented. For each, the same points of comparison are made (student population, special services, recent enrollment patterns), giving the reader an overall picture of each college.

---

*When we are asked to *compare* two things, we often include both similarities and differences. However, when we *contrast*, we focus on differences.

Point-by-point: The same information could be presented in a different way if the writer wanted to stress the differences. The *point-by-point* method is used in this outline of the same material. The Roman numerals mark the three points that the author wants to make about the two colleges. The capital letters indicate the order in which the colleges will be discussed. Again, notice that the same order is used under each section.

> **Thesis: Although Hammond College and Williamsburg College share similarities as "community colleges," they are different in several ways.**

I. Student population
   - A.   Hammond College
   - B.   Williamsburg College

II. Special services
   - A.   Hammond College
   - B.   Williamsburg College

III. Recent enrollment patterns
   - A.   Hammond College
   - B.   Williamsburg College

To decide which of these two methods to use when planning an essay, consider the nature of the topic and the sophistication of the reader. If the topic has a lot of detail, the point-by-point method would probably be better because it lends itself to more detailed development of the topic. The item-by-item organization is good for more limited topics. It is less satisfactory for more complex topics, however, because the writer has to continually refer to items in previous paragraphs, or the reader has to make the connections.

Exercise 5. Outlining a Reading I

The following student essay compares two short essays taken from longer writings by two well-known authors, Helen Keller ("My Most Important Day") and Rudolfo Anaya ("Antonio's First Day at School"). In their stories, each author describes an important day in her or his life. The writer of the essay, Jorge Hernandez, compares and contrasts the ways in which the two stories are related.

Read the essay carefully. Then discuss it in groups or with your teacher to identify the thesis and the topic ideas of the paragraphs. Decide whether the author follows an item-by-item or a point-by-point pattern for the comparison and prepare an outline. Keep your outline for writing a summary later in this chapter.

Important Childhood Events

Most of us at some time in our lives experience an event that will never vanish from our minds. "My Most Important Day," by Helen Keller, and "Antonio's First Day at School," by Rudolfo Anaya, are alike in many ways. In both short essays, the authors relate a childhood event that had a great effect on their later lives.

In both stories, the event was one of the most important in the author's life. For Helen Keller, the event was the time that her friend and teacher, Anne Sullivan, first came to help her. Before Helen met Anne Sullivan, she was a bewildered, blind deaf mute, unable to communicate with the rest of the world. With the help of Anne Sullivan, she was able to learn to communicate and was released from her sightless, soundless world. Rudolfo, likewise, in the autobiographical story "Antonio's First Day at School," shares with the reader his first experience in learning, the first day when he left the warmth of his home and the protection of his mother. The feelings he experienced on that first day stayed with him all of his life. Both authors always remembered these early childhood events.

In both cases, the memorable event had to do with the authors' educations. In Helen's case, education was informal; she was taught at home by Anne Sullivan, who was hired by her parents from the Perkins School for the Blind. Her patient, kind teacher worked with the unruly Helen until she finally understood the meanings of words through the finger spelling that she was being taught. With much difficulty, Helen learned to communicate. Rudolfo (Antonio), on the other hand, had a formal education, away from his family, in a public school. He was removed from the warmth of his family and the protection of his mother; on his first day of school, he found himself required to understand and learn a new language: English. Rudolfo was forced to band together with other non-English-speaking students to overcome his feelings of loneliness in school, but, like Helen, he too learned a new means of communication.

Both authors felt a deep loneliness and loss at this time in their lives. Helen felt like "a ship at sea in a dense fog, shut in by a tangible white darkness." She cried quietly for "Light!" She was "without compass and had no way of knowing how near the harbor was." Likewise, Rudolfo yearned for his mother and felt like an outcast. He wanted to run away and hide. These feelings were a result of an inability to communicate—Helen because of her physical handicap and Rudolfo because of the language barrier.

In the end, both authors overcame their difficulties. Helen's understanding of the world around her "awakened her soul, gave it light, hope and joy and set her free." Rudolfo found others who had his same problem and by banding together with them was able to overcome his struggle to stay in school and not return home to shame his family's name. For both authors, then, the childhood event was important. Rudolfo never forgot that feeling of loneliness, which he never again shared with anyone as he had with his classmates. Helen never forgot the meaning that Anne Sullivan gave to her life through the gift of communication.

Jorge Hernandez
Student

Exercise 6. Outlining a Reading II

 The author of the following essay compares and contrasts English and his language, Indonesian. Read the essay carefully, identify the thesis idea and main ideas, and decide whether the author follows an item-by-item or a point-by-point pattern of organization. Prepare an outline.

Differences in Communication

Many of my difficulties in learning English result from the differences that exist between my language, Indonesian, and English. These differences are of two basic types. First, there are the obvious differences in grammar and syntax; however, there are also differences in the nonverbal systems of communication, which may not be as immediately observable but which are just as important for getting a message across. Both of these systems, verbal and nonverbal, are governed by rules that must be learned in order for communication to take place.

Actually, Indonesian and English have very similar sentence patterns, with the subject coming first in a sentence and the predicate and object following it. But there the similarity ends. In forming questions, the patterns are not the same at all. Also, in Indonesian, there are no tenses; we write all sentences with the verb in the same form regardless of changes in time. For instance, in English, we use the simple present tense to express something done again and again or a habit, as in the sentence, "I go to school every day." Also, we change the verb "go" to "went" when we want to use a past time. In Indonesian, however, we never make any changes in the verbs, but add other words to show time. For example, we say "I go to school *every day*" and "I go to school *yesterday.*" Whereas in English we have problems with subject-verb agreement, having to be careful not to say "they comes" but "they come," in Indonesian we don't have any such required verb changes. Thus, Indonesian students may have a terrible time with the English verb system.

The most difficult problem Indonesians commonly face with English grammar is the use of articles, since there are no specific articles in our language. I have to consider whether the noun is count or noncount, whether it is specific, general, or generic, or whether, if it is a proper noun, it takes an article or not. Then I must choose between *a* and *an* depending on whether the noun begins with a consonant or vowel sound. Since Indonesian doesn't have such a system, most students have a hard time remembering to use articles at all, much less use them correctly.

In addition to these verbal variations, differences can also be found in the nonverbal forms of communication in Indonesia and the United States. One example can be found in gestures, which in all cultures carry various meanings. In both Indonesia and the United States, one can see the "thumbs up" gesture, and the perceived meaning in both cases is very positive. In the United States, it may mean everything is "okay," while in Indonesia, it means that you have done a good job or you are a good person. Another gesture used in both countries is the extension of the finger in a V-shape. After World War II, people made that sign for "Victory," and now in the United States it is used for "Victory" or "Peace." In Indonesia, that symbol simply means the number "two." Another similar symbol is the "o" shape formed by the thumb and the first finger. In the United States, if someone makes that sign for you, you have done well and should be proud of yourself. However, in Indonesia, if that signal is given to you (especially after a test), you will feel sorry or ashamed because that symbol only means "zero."

Although most people never think about this, space is another aspect of communication, and Americans traveling in Indonesia might be a little surprised at the different concept of where one person stands in relation to another. For example, an Indonesian man will rarely hug a woman in public; men and women usually just shake hands. Men, on the other hand, often walk with their arms around each other and hug each other upon meeting. Americans find this behavior very different from their own, and if they are unaware of our Indonesian customs, they may misjudge the men involved.

Fortunately, during my stay in the United States so far, I have not made any embarrassing mistakes in either verbal or nonverbal communication around Americans, but this may be because I am very aware that many differences exist which I must be careful of. It is advisable for anyone who plans to spend time in a foreign country to learn about differences in the verbal communication systems as well as culturally bound variations in the nonverbal systems of the native and foreign cultures.

Swie Siong Tio
Student

PREPARATION FOR WRITING: Using Facts and Statistics from Charts and Graphs

The first writing assignment later in this lesson will require you to compare two colleges using facts and statistics presented in different types of graphs and charts. To use such information, you must first understand the graph or chart and then translate that information into verbal form for writing. To prepare for that, we'll do two exercises that will require you to write a paragraph using information from charts or graphs.

When using charts and graphs:

1. Find the title of the graph or chart to see what information is given.
2. See if there is a key on the graph; it will tell you what the dots, lines, and symbols mean.
3. On a bar or a line graph, look at the numbers along the bottom or side to see what variables are used.
4. Summarize the information on the graph or chart by translating the information into written form.
    • Express the main idea.
    • Support it with details from the chart.

Exercise 7. Writing a Paragraph Using Information from a Pie Chart

A graph in the form of a circle is often called a pie chart. With a partner, look at the following pie chart and answer the questions that follow it.

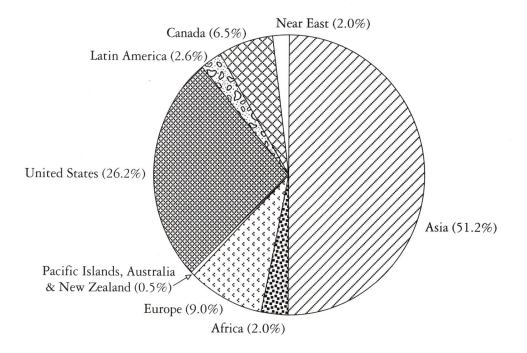

Figure 4.1
TOEFL Registrations by Region—1990-1991
Reprinted by permission of Educational Testing Service.

1. What is the title? (TOEFL is an acronym for "Test of English as a Foreign Language.")

   _____

   _____

2. What is compared?

   _____

   _____

3. What conclusions can you draw from the graph? In what region do the most TOEFL registrations occur? The fewest?

   _____

   _____

   _____

   _____

   _____

After you have drawn conclusions from the graph, write a paragraph titled, "Worldwide TOEFL Registrations." Write a topic sentence and then use the following details in addition to figures from the graph. Where will you include the information from the graph?

Be sure to start your paragraph with a topic sentence!

- About 3,000 educational institutions in the United States, Canada, and other English-speaking countries require TOEFL scores.
- Tests are now given at more then 1,200 centers in 170 countries.
- More than 670,000 candidates took the TOEFL in 1990-91.

Exercise 8. Writing a Paragraph Using Information from Bar and Line Graphs

Working with a partner, look at the following perpendicular bar graph and answer the questions.

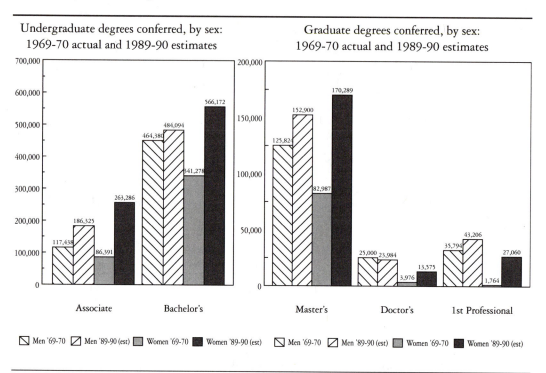

Undergraduate degrees conferred, by sex: 1969-70 actual and 1989-90 estimates

Graduate degrees conferred, by sex: 1969-70 actual and 1989-90 estimates

Source: *Early Estimates, National Higher Education Statistics: Fall 1990,* published by the National Center for Education Statistics, Office of Educational Research and Improvement, U.S. Department of Education

Figure 4.2
Charting the Course

1. What is compared in each graph?

   _____

   _____

2. What do the numbers at the left of each graph represent?

   _____

   _____

3. What do the lines and the shaded areas in the rectangles represent?

   _____

   _____

4. What conclusions can you draw from these graphs? (draw at least five, and more if you can)

   _____

   _____

   _____

   _____

   _____

Now look at the following line graph and answer the questions.

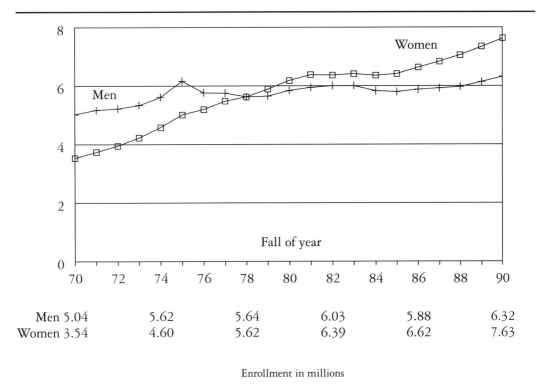

Men 5.04	5.62	5.64	6.03	5.88	6.32
Women 3.54	4.60	5.62	6.39	6.62	7.63

Enrollment in millions

Source: *Early Estimates, National Higher Education Statistics: Fall 1990,* published by the National Center for Education Statistics, Office of Educational Research and Improvement, U.S. Department of Education

Figure 4.3
Enrollments in Institutions of Higher Education by Sex

1. What is compared in this line graph?

   _____

   _____

2. What do the numbers at the left of the graph represent?

   _____

   _____

3. What do the numbers across the bottom of the graph represent?

   _____

   _____

4. What do the numbers below the graph represent?

_____

_____

5. What conclusions can you draw from this graph? (draw at least two, and more if you can)

_____

_____

_____

_____

_____

6. Why is a line graph effective in presenting this information?

_____

_____

_____

Write a paragraph: Using conclusions drawn from the graphs, write a paragraph comparing and contrasting the enrollment of men and women in institutions of higher education in the United States from 1969-1990. Support your conclusions with details (facts and figures) from the graphs.

_____

_____

_____

_____

_____

_____

Exercise 9. Writing a Paragraph Using Information from a Horizontal Bar Graph

With a partner look at the horizontal bar graph on the following page and answer the questions.

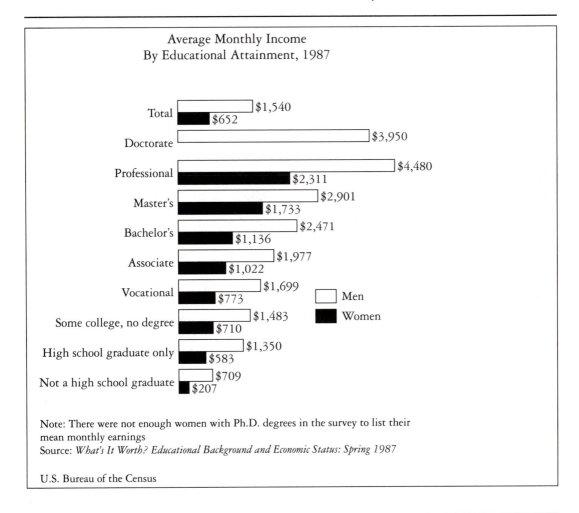

Figure 4.4
Educational Background and Economic Status

1. What is compared in this horizontal bar graph?

   _____

   _____

2. What do the dollar amounts to the right of each bar represent?

   _____

   _____

3. What two major conclusions can you draw from this graph?

   _____

   _____

   _____

   _____

   _____

Write a paragraph: Write a paragraph in which you answer the question, "Does education really pay off?" Use facts and figures from the graph to support your conclusion.

STRUCTURE REVIEW: Reported Speech

There are two ways to report what someone else said. One way is to quote the person's words directly.

Mr. Meridian said, "I want to run for political office."

The other way is to paraphrase the person's words by using *reported speech.*

Mr. Meridian said that he wanted to run for political office.

Note these differences between quoted (or direct) speech and reported (indirect) speech.

1. *Differences in sentence structure*

Direct speech: Mrs. Holland said, "It is snowing hard."

The first part of the sentence includes, as the subject, the person making the statement (*Mrs. Holland*), and the verb of reporting, questioning, or commanding (*said*). The second part is an independent clause which is the exact statement made by the subject of the first clause.

Reported Speech: Mrs. Holland said that it was snowing hard.

Reported speech has an independent clause and a dependent clause (*that it was snowing hard.*). The dependent clause follows a verb of reporting (in this case, *said*).

2. *Differences in punctuation*

In reported speech, there is no comma after the verb of reporting, and the quotation marks are dropped. In a reported question or command, a question mark or an exclamation point becomes a period because the new sentence no longer includes an independent question or imperative. It is a *report* of a previously formed question or command.

The instructor said, "The test will be Tuesday."

The instructor told us the test would be Tuesday.

The police officer asked, "Is he the robber?"

The police officer asked if he was the robber.

3. *Differences in verb tenses*

In both direct and reported speech, the verb of reporting is often in the past tense because the report is made *after the original statement.*

Bill *said,* "It is raining."

Bill *said* that it was raining.

The verb in the reported speech is often (but not always) changed to a past form.

Bill said, "It *is* raining."

Bill said that it *was* raining.

Barbara told John, "I *will* marry you."

Barbara told John that she *would* marry him. (*Would* is the past form of *will.*)

If the original verb is a past form modal such as *might* or *could,* no change is made.

Susan stated, "I *might go* to the party."

Susan stated that she *might* go to the party.

If the original verb is already in the past tense, it is changed to past perfect.

Professor Carlson reported, "I *gave* the lecture at 8:00 last night."

Professor Carlson reported that he *had given* the lecture at 8:00 the previous night.

This follows the rules for usage of the past perfect tense to describe an action or state occurring before another past action or state. Professor Carlson must first give the lecture before he can report the fact. In formal written English, this tense change rule is usually followed except when the reported statement expresses a universal or general truth, in which case the verb may remain in the present tense.

The science teacher explained that water *boils* at 212° F.

4. *Differences in pronouns*

    The pronoun in the reported clause may have to change to refer to the person making the report.

    Mrs. Smith said, "*I* can call you later."

    Mrs. Smith said that *she* could call later.

5. *Differences in adverbs*

    Sometimes adverbs (words relating to time) require changes to make them refer to the appropriate day or date.

    The forecaster predicted, "It will rain *tomorrow.*"

    The forecaster predicted that it would rain *the next day*.

6. *Joining words*

    There is usually a "joining" word between the verb of reporting and the dependent clause. In statements, the joining word *that* is usually inserted before the verb of reporting and the dependent clause, but it is sometimes omitted.

Mrs. Hershey said, "I will be late."

Mrs. Hershey said (*that*) she would be late.

In reported *yes/no* questions, the joining word is *if* or *whether*, and the clause takes statement word order.

The president asked, "Will the senators vote for this bill?"

The president asked *if* (*whether*) the senators would vote for the bill.

In *wh-* questions, the joining word is the interrogative word (*who, what, when, how, why, where*) and the clause takes statement word order.

The environmentalist asked, "Why do we permit industries to pollute our rivers?"

The environmentalist asked why we permitted industries to pollute our rivers.

In reported commands, the independent command clause is converted into an infinitive phrase.

The Surgeon General has warned the public, "Don't smoke!"

The Surgeon General has warned the public *not to smoke*.

Exercise 1. Restating with Reported Speech I

Read the conversation between Ahmed, a student in an English class, and Dr. Mathews, the professor. Then report the conversation. Omit any unnecessary words or phrases as you report the conversation.

1. Dr. Mathews: I'd like to talk about your last essay, Ahmed.
2. Ahmed: I spent a lot of time on it.
3. Dr. Mathews: Did you go to the library for some of your information?
4. Ahmed: Yes. The librarian helped me with the resources.
5. Dr. Mathews: Have you ever had to write a research paper before?
6. Ahmed: No, I haven't.
7. Dr. Mathews: Well, there are some problems with your essay. You've copied information directly from other sources without giving references.
8. Ahmed: Is that wrong?
9. Dr. Mathews: Yes. If you do that, you'll be accused of plagiarizing. Teachers won't accept plagiarized work.
10. Ahmed: I guess I'd better learn how to do it right.
11. Dr. Mathews: That's a good idea.
12. Ahmed: Do you teach a course in writing research papers?
13. Dr. Mathews: Yes. You can take that course next semester.

Reported speech:

1. Dr. Mathews told Ahmed _____

   _____

2. Ahmed said_____

   _____

3. Dr. Mathews asked Ahmed _____

   _____

4. Ahmed said yes and that _____

   _____

5. Dr. Mathews asked _____

   _____

6. Ahmed replied _____

   _____

7. Dr. Mathews said that _____

   _____

   and that _____

   _____

8. Ahmed asked _____

   _____

9. Dr. Mathews told Ahmed that _____

   _____

   and that _____

   _____

10. Ahmed was worried and said that _____

    _____

11. Dr. Mathews said _____

    _____

12. Ahmed asked Dr. Mathews _____

    _____

13. Dr. Mathews told Ahmed _____

    _____

Exercise 2. Restating with Reported Speech II

Read the following paragraphs. *Restate* the author's ideas by using what you have learned about reported speech to answer the questions following each passage. Do not include any words or phrases that are not necessary to convey the author's basic ideas.

1. The U. S. government's system of "checks and balances" is not the most efficient type, but it is the fairest. Sometimes it takes a long time for a good idea to be put into practice because it must be debated in Congress, approved by the executive branch (the president), and often reviewed by the Supreme Court. The principle of democracy is very evident in this system of cross-checking. No one person or governmental branch can ever acquire all of the power for making and enforcing the laws of the land.

    a. What did the author claim about the fairness of the system of "checks and balances"?

    The author claimed _____

    _____

    b. What did the author state about the principle of democracy?

    The author stated _____

    _____

    c. According to the author, can one person ever acquire all of the law-making power under the U. S. system?

    The author explained _____

    _____

2. One of the mainstays of a democracy is the right of all citizens to a free public education. This ensures to each citizen the possibility of attaining his or her potential and is absolutely essential to develop an informed electorate. However, any system that requires that all people be included will have weaknesses. One such weakness is the amount of money that must be spent to educate the masses; in order to raise funds for public schools, millions of dollars must be obtained by federal and state governments in the form of taxes. This means that even taxpayers without children must share the cost of schooling for all. However, in my opinion, a much more serious weakness is the loss of quality inherent in any mass education program. If the least capable students must be educated alongside the most intelligent and motivated, there will be a leveling of the standards and educational requirements. The most able students will not be challenged to work up to their capacity. Thus, since teachers must direct their energy

toward the students in the middle ranges of intelligence, the system leads to general mediocrity.

a. What did the author say was a "mainstay of a democracy"?

The author said _____

_____

b. What was the first weakness the author claimed was inherent in the system?

The author claimed _____

_____

c. What did the author state about childless taxpayers?

The author stated _____

_____

d. What is a more serious weakness in the system?

The author thinks _____

_____

e. Why will the most intelligent and capable students be harmed by this system?

The author claimed _____

_____

f. Does this system lead to a high level of quality in the classroom, according to the author?

The author believes _____

_____

Exercise 3. Reporting a Conversation

Interview a classmate about his or her views on one of the topics below or on a topic of your own choosing. First, make a list of questions that you want to ask. Take notes during the interview so that you will have a record of what your classmate answered. After completing the interview, write a paragraph *reporting* what your classmate said.

1. Intercultural marriages
2. The role of women in society
3. The ideal career
4. The advantages of any system of government (democracy, monarchy, etc.)
5. Free public education for all citizens

WRITING ASSIGNMENT ONE:
Writing a Comparison Together

For this assignment three classmates are to write an essay comparing Hammond College and Williamsburg College. The charts and graphs that follow give information comparing the two colleges.

Prewriting activity: First, discuss the information in each chart or graph with your classmates. You may want to look back at the section, "Preparation for Writing: Using Facts and Statistics from Charts and Graphs," on pages 111–118. From your analysis, draw conclusions about the two colleges. Use these generalizations for topic ideas for your essay.

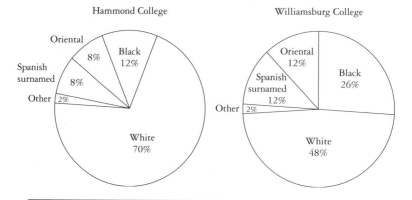

Figure 4.5 Number of Students by Ethnic Group Distribution

Conclusions:

_____

_____

_____

_____

	Hammond College	Williamsburg College
Career Counseling	Yes	Yes
Tuition Assistance	Yes	Yes
Basic Skills Courses	No	Yes
Recruitment in Local High Schools	No	Yes
Child-care for Students	Yes	No
Assistance for Displaced	No	Yes
Tutorial Services	Yes	Yes
English as a Second Language	No	Yes

Figure 4.6
Special Services Offered

Conclusions:

_____

_____

_____

_____

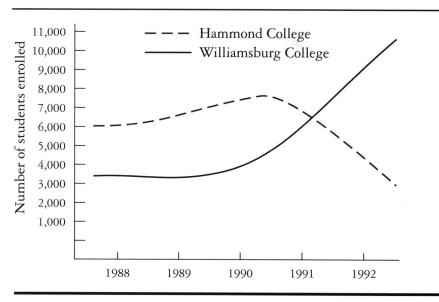

Figure 4.7
Five–year Enrollment Pattern

Conclusions:

_____

_____

_____

_____

Decide on a thesis for your essay: What conclusions have you drawn about these two colleges after looking at the chart and the graphs? Does one college seem to be doing better than the other? Do you have any idea why? Which college would you choose to attend? Why?

Use the conclusions you have drawn about the colleges to formulate a thesis statement:

Thesis:

_____

_____

_____

Decide on an organizational pattern: Look back at the outlines at the beginning of this chapter for two possibilities for organizing your essay.

Write the introduction with your classmates: You might want to include the following similarities between the two colleges in your introduction.

- Both colleges are located in the same metropolitan area.
- Both are easily accessible by bus lines.
- Both are about 20 years old.
- Both have reasonably priced tuition.

Write the body: Each student is to write one body paragraph of the essay, including relevant information from the charts and graphs for support. One is to write about number of students by race or ethnic group, one is to write about special services offered, and one is to write about the enrollment patterns.

Write the conclusion with your classmates: Try to make some predictions about the future of these two colleges, based on the information you gathered from the charts and graphs. What do you think will happen to the two colleges in the future? What do you think the colleges should do to prepare for the future?

Read and revise the essay: Each writer is to read the essay and make suggestions for revision of any part. The group should decide on final revisions.

Read and edit the essay: Each writer is to read the essay for errors in spelling, punctuation, grammar, and sentence structure before the final draft is written.

WRITING ASSIGNMENT TWO:

Writing a Comparison on Your Own

Write a composition on any of the following topics (or a topic assigned by your instructor). These topics will require that you use some form of comparison and contrast pattern organization.

Incorporate what you have learned about writing essays into this assignment: gathering ideas, organizing (outlining), writing introductions and conclusions, and using connecting words.

Follow the steps in the writing process: discuss your topic with classmates or others; write the first draft; share your draft with classmates for feedback; revise; edit your draft for errors in punctuation, grammar, and sentence structure.

Topics:

- Two world leaders
- Two forms of government

- Lecture (history) vs. lab (biology) classes
- ESL/EFL vs. academic classes
- Typing vs. word processing
- Buying a house (or apartment) vs. renting one
- Problems in a developing and a developed country
- An Oriental and a Western religion

SUMMARY WRITING
Part Four: Paraphrasing Ideas

Paraphrasing is restating an author's ideas using different words and phrases instead of quoting an author exactly. The author's essential point is kept, but the vocabulary (using synonyms) or the sentence structure (changing from active to passive or changing the clause structure) may be changed.

The following sentences have been paraphrased by changing words, phrases, and sentence structures. Read each one and, with your teacher, determine what changes have been made.

"The individual who lacks affection, recognition or the fulfillment of other emotional needs may turn to food."

A person who is unloved or unrecognized may eat for emotional fulfillment.

"Education in the United States is financed by taxing everyone, even those people without children or those whose children attend private school."

Even childless people or those with children in private schools contribute to education through taxes in the United States.

"Computer systems contain internal memory units for storage of instructions and data; in addition, they may include external systems to increase the memory and provide flexibility."

Instructions and data are kept in the internal memory units of computer systems. External memory units may be added for extra storage and flexibility.

Exercise 1. Paraphrasing Sentences

Following the examples above, rewrite each sentence twice. In *a* use the word form in parentheses. In *b* find a synonymous phrase and rewrite the sentence. In most cases you will have to make structural changes also. The first has been done for you.

(*Note to the teacher:* These exercises are best to do on the board with the whole class and then in smaller groups until students seem to understand the process of paraphrasing clearly.)

1. The modern dog is *descended* from a wolflike animal, the tomarctus.

   a. (*a descendant*) *The dog is a descendant of a wolflike animal, the tomarctus.*

   _____

   b. *The tomarctus, a wolflike animal, is the ancestor of the dog.*

   _____

2. There is *evidence* that trained dogs hunted with primitive man as early as 10,000 B.C.

    a. (*evidently*) _____

    _____

    b. _____

    _____

3. Early elite Egyptians, who first kept dogs as pets, even had servants to *attend* them.

    a. (*attending*) _____

    _____

    b. _____

    _____

4. Early Greeks used dogs to *track* lions in Africa.

    a. (*for tracking*) _____

    _____

    b. _____

    _____

5. Dogs have been *employed to serve* mankind for centuries.

    a. (*in the employment*) _____

    _____

    b. _____

    _____

6. Elephants *evolved* from a large prehistoric animal, the mammoth, to be the world's largest land animal.

    a. (*evolving*) _____

    _____

    b. _____

    _____

7. The elephant is known for its *superior* brain and *submissive* disposition.

    a. (*superiority/submissiveness*) _____

    _____

    b. _____

    _____

8. Despite their *massive* size, elephants are known for being *agile.*

   a. (*massiveness/agility*) _____

   _____

   b. _____

   _____

9. Elephants have often been sought for food and for their *valuable* ivory tusks.

   a. (*value*) _____

   _____

   b. _____

   _____

10. Because elephants *consume* up to 500 pounds of food a day, they are able to strip a forest bare in no time.

    a. (*consumption*) _____

    _____

    b. _____

    _____

11. Lions, *sharing* origins with the domestic cat, appeared on earth and roamed the jungle.

    a. (*share*) _____

    _____

    b. _____

    _____

12. Over the centuries, lions have been used in art to *represent* power and magnificence.

    a. (*representing*) _____

    _____

    b. _____

    _____

13. Lions are social animals with one *dominant* male in each pride. (A *pride* is a group of lions.)

    a. (*dominate*) _____

    _____

b. _____

_____

14. Females show great *affection* for cubs, even those that are not their own.

a. (*affectionate*) _____

_____

b. _____

_____

15. Lions are very *intelligent* and at times even *humorous*.

a. (*intelligence/humor*) _____

_____

b. _____

_____

Exercise 2. Paraphrasing Authors' Words

Paraphrase each sentence. There may be more than one way to rewrite each one. Remember to change vocabulary, phrases, and sentence structures wherever you can.

1. George Washington Carver was a dedicated teacher; in addition, he was known as a talented artist, musician, and researcher who made valuable contributions to his people and his country.

_____

_____

_____

2. Archibald MacLeish, known for his poetry, was appointed head of the Library of Congress by President Roosevelt in 1939.

_____

_____

_____

3. Newspaper writers are responsible for reporting the news clearly, correctly, and objectively, and for giving facts rather than opinions.

_____

_____

_____

4. Legends tell of an ancient civilization called Atlantis, which was blown apart by a tremendous explosion and destroyed thirty-five hundred years ago.

_____

_____

_____

5. The jojoba, a plant that grows wild in the dry areas of the southwestern United States and northern Mexico, produces a valuable oil that can be used in cosmetics and machine lubricants.

_____

_____

_____

6. Although it is not always easy to tell the difference between folk art and fine art, each has distinctive characteristics that help to identify it.

_____

_____

_____

7. For many Americans, the automobile is not only a necessity but also a convenience.

_____

_____

_____

8. P. T. Barnum, founder of the famous Barnum and Bailey Circus, became famous for his huge circus tent and for his sarcastic sayings.

_____

_____

_____

9. The United States House of Representatives includes 435 representatives, each of whom is elected by people of a particular "district" or area in each state.

_____

_____

_____

10. As the possession of nuclear weapons spreads to more and more nations, there is a much greater possibility of nuclear war.

_____

_____

_____

Exercise 3. Writing Main Idea Sentences

Read each paragraph and state the main idea in your own words. If you find the main idea stated directly in the paragraph, be sure to use the paraphrasing techniques that you practiced in Exercises 1 and 2.

1. There is plenty of water on the earth. In fact, there is enough water on this planet for everyone to have a huge lake. The trouble is that the water isn't always found in the place where it is needed. In addition, much of the water is polluted or salty. Because of these problems, there are many people without sufficient water.

Main idea _____

_____

_____

2. New oil supplies need to be found to replace those that have been used up. There is a constant search for new oil fields. Oil hunters sink their wells wherever there are signs of oil. Each of these drillings costs thousands and thousands of dollars, and often there isn't enough oil to make it profitable. Nevertheless, the search for new oil never ends.

Main idea _____

_____

_____

3. Quakers, a religious group known as the Society of Friends, have always worked for humane causes. Before the Civil War in the United States, they were against slavery and led the movement to help slaves escape from the southern part of the United States and seek freedom in the northern part. Today, they fight hunger and disease around the globe and still aid people fleeing tyranny and war. Their beliefs are based on the principles of pacifism and simple living.

Main idea _____

_____

_____

4. American Indians originally migrated from the Bering Strait down through North America and into South America. After thousands of years of migration, they developed highly advanced levels of civilization. Indians in the Ohio valley created beautifully carved objects and built strange mounds over burial areas. Indians in the Southwest constructed apartment-like dwellings which are still used. Maya and Aztec Indians in Mexico crafted extraordinary gold jewelry, and the Incas of Peru developed skills in mathematics and astronomy that amaze us today.

    Main idea _____

    _____

    _____

5. Early immigrants to the United States, in an effort to build the new nation, quickly became absorbed into the new society. It was believed that the United States would be a "melting pot" into which all newcomers would blend into one strong nation. However, when the later immigrants from Europe came, they settled in their own ethnic neighborhoods where they retained their culture and customs in places such as New York's "Chinatown" and "Little Italy." Later, their children learned American ways and rejected the old ways. Today the attitude has changed; people have become interested in their pasts, and it is now believed that society will benefit by retaining aspects of the cultural backgrounds of its new citizens.

    Main idea _____

    _____

    _____

6. In the mid-18th century, a formal system of sign language was developed to help deaf people communicate. A French clergyman and educator of the deaf, Charles Michel, first developed a system for spelling words with a manual alphabet and later expanded his system to include whole concepts. Later in 1816, Thomas Gallaudet, an American educator, introduced it into the United States, and it became known as American Sign Language. Like all spoken languages, ASL is constantly changing, but it continues to serve more than 500,000 deaf people in the United States and Canada in the same basic form as was developed by Gallaudet.

    Main idea _____

    _____

    _____

7. For many years, genealogy (the investigation of ancestry and family histories) was mainly undertaken by upper-class Americans seeking to prove their relation to royalty or to early patriots. Now, searching for one's ancestors has become a popular avocation; however, a genealogical search is usually not easy. Records are often hard to locate, and the information may not be reliable when found. Often names were changed on census or other forms for various reasons, and indifferent clerks who recorded information often made errors. The spelling of names has been ever-changing, with immigration officials often spelling names phonetically, and our own foreign forefathers often anglicized their names themselves upon reaching this land. But if one persists at the search, ancestor-hunting has great rewards. Whether we find our ancestors were princes or paupers, it helps us develop an appreciation for those who have gone before us.

Main idea _____

_____

_____

Chapter Five
Focus on Content: Cause and Effect Analysis

ORGANIZING A CAUSE/EFFECT ANALYSIS

Just as with comparison and contrast, the analysis of *cause and effect* is something we do every day. We may have to make a decision about a job change or a move for our family, and before we make our choice, we consider all the effects it will have on us. Likewise, we often ponder the causes of some event. We may wonder why we lost a job or why a friend has not called, and we search for causes.

On a more formal level, we use a lot of *cause/effect analysis* in our pursuit of education. In a science class, we may be asked to write down the causes and effects of a certain scientific experiment; in our history class, we may be asked to give the causes of World War II or consider its effects on the world; in our psychology class, we may be asked to discuss the causes of a certain emotional disorder and the effect of different kinds of therapy. Cause/effect analysis, then, is a common analytical skill used far beyond the writing class.

In developing a cause/effect essay, we have to analyze causes and effects that are both immediate (recent in time or very directly related to the topic) and remote (farther away in time or less directly related). Considering the nature of the subject, we must decide whether we want to emphasize cause or effect, or if we should place equal emphasis on both. We must often consider the relationships between causes and effects since in some cases one effect may also be a cause, with an effect of its own, as in a chain reaction. The following exercises will provide practice in working with cause/effect analysis.

Exercise 1. Cause/Effect

Look at these thesis statements. Decide whether the emphasis in each one is on the *cause* or the *effect* of something. The first statement has been done for you.

_____*cause*_____ 1. Accidents at home are usually the result of carelessness.

_____ 2. As a result of a heart attack, the victim may have physical activities limited, suffer a degeneration of other body activities, or even die.

_____ 3. My friend lost his job because of his poor work performance and his inability to get along with other workers.

——————————— 4. TV viewers can suffer from both eye strain and intellectual boredom.

——————————— 5. Poverty and our nation's inability to share the wealth have been pointed out as the reasons why people in our society turn to crime.

——————————— 6. On a trip to Brazil, I observed how the climate has affected its economy, architecture, and people.

——————————— 7. The occurrence of a third world war will probably be the result of our leaders' inability to communicate with each other and the military's constant desire for more advanced military weapons.

——————————— 8. Houseplants die for a variety of reasons, including lack of sufficient sunlight and water.

Exercise 2. Brainstorming Ideas: Effects in Chain Reactions

Many events can cause a chain reaction. For example, suppose you lost your job. There would be many effects, some of which would be the causes for other effects, such as the following.

Cause: loss of job

Effect 1:   loss of income
                    ↓
              inability to pay the rent/mortgage
                    ↓
                  loss of home
                    ↓
                moving in with relatives
                    ↓
                  family tensions

Effect 2:   loss of daily structure
                    ↓
                  boredom

Effect 3:   loss of self-esteem
                    ↓
                  depression
                    ↓
                no confidence in finding a new job

Now, with a partner or a small group, give as many effects as you can of the following situations. As you write down your effects, notice whether any of them is the cause of another effect (called a "chain reaction").

1. You move from a large house with a yard to a small apartment.
2. You leave the small town where you grew up and knew everyone to move to a large city.
3. You lose your eyesight.
4. You get married.
5. You win a lottery.
6. You lose your credit card.

Did you find any examples of chain reactions as you made your lists?

Exercise 3. Brainstorming Ideas: Causes

With a partner or a small group, think of as many causes as you can for the following hypothetical situations.

1. A car accident.
2. A person's loss of a job.
3. A student's failure to pass a course.
4. The closing of a school.
5. A person's getting elected to public office.
6. Immigration.

Exercise 4. Ordering Ideas

Causes and effects can be ordered in several ways, including *chain order,* *chronological order,* and *order of importance.* In each of the following, read the thesis and decide on the best order for the supporting ideas. Number them 1, 2, 3, and so on. For each set, be able to indicate which principle of order you have used. Are there any lists that have more than one possible order?

1. **Thesis: Scientists predict a food crisis of great proportion in the next century unless population growth is curtailed.**

_____ Most important, even when enough food is grown, the problem of the cost of distributing it to needy people in the world exists.

_____ Population increases by about 100 million yearly. Agricultural output cannot keep up with the need.

_____ The cost of farm machinery, the oil to run it, and the technology to improve agriculture are at present prohibitive.

_____ Also, agricultural production depends on suitable weather, which is both unpredictable and uncontrollable.

2. **Thesis: The action of air both inside and outside the ear causes us to hear sound.**

_____ Inside the eardrum, a system of small bones vibrates to amplify the movements on the surface of the eardrum.

_____ Air moves outside the head to vibrate the eardrum, which is a membrane of tissue.

_____ These cells send the impulses to the brain, which then decodes the signals into what we hear.

_____ These bones connect to a snail-like section filled with fluid, which is agitated to stimulate nerve cells.

3. **Thesis: Many colleges and universities are having financial problems because of the high rate of unemployment.**

_____ The most obvious effect of unemployment is that people cannot afford to send their children to college.

_____ Just as important but less obvious is the fact that with fewer people working, fewer taxes are paid. As a result, states have less money to aid education.

_____ Also, students themselves cannot find jobs to help finance their own education.

_____ In addition, states spend more on social services, such as unemployment compensation, and less on education.

4. **Thesis: There have been many reasons for the immigration of people from other countries to the United States.**

_____ In this century, immigrants from Mexico and Central America have come mostly for economic reasons.

_____ The first European immigrants in the seventeenth and eighteenth centuries came seeking religious freedom and equality.

_____ During the late nineteenth and early twentieth centuries, immigrants fled from poverty-stricken countries of Europe, such as Ireland and Poland.

_____ Blacks were unwilling immigrants to America, having been brought from Africa as slaves in the eighteenth century.

Exercise 5. Essay Analysis

Read the following two essays, which express opinions about modern American education, and answer the questions that follow each.

A Nation of Illiterates?

Has the electronic age turned our children into a nation of highly technological but culturally illiterate people? This question is being debated at parent-teacher organizations, neighborhood groups and family dinner tables. The invention of television has been widely blamed for the short attention spans of our students in school as well as a decline in the reading done by most school-aged children. However, the more recent video games, computerized information searches, and other electronic inventions seem to threaten the cultural level of the world's citizens even further with effects that will reach far into the future.

Observe the average high school student today. He rushes off for the school bus, toting his computer-generated term paper in fulfillment of a class project while plugged in to his favorite rock star by means of a portable tape or compact disc player. In "writing" his term paper, he has made use of an encyclopedic search program on his personal computer and a graphics design program to make his work more attractive. He does not even have to be able to spell, for the spell-check program of his word processor takes that burden off his shoulders.

Arriving at school, he carries his pocket calculator that can perform any of the more sophisticated operations needed in his math class. Mention the technical wizard of his parents' generation, the slide rule, and almost certainly he will have no idea what you are talking about. Learn multiplication tables? Why? The answer is always at his fingertips, and no careless human mistakes will lower his math grade.

In English class, our favorite teen sleeps through the lesson on "Hamlet" (after all, he can always rent the Mel Gibson version at the video store) and smiles ironically when the teacher encourages "reading for pleasure." Why should he read when there is so much entertainment that requires no thought or imagination on his part? Besides, it takes a lot of time to plow through all those pages, and he has scheduled a video game tournament with his friends after school. Everyone knows those contests can last for hours. Even the fairy tales and children's classics that his parents used to read to him when he was a toddler have become confused, in his mind, with the television and movie versions.

Just one more class to get through until he can escape into "real life." History class. Yawn. What a bore! Who cares about the industrial revolution when compared with the incredible achievements in the field of technology he has seen during his brief lifetime? Hasn't that teacher walked outside of the classroom once in recent years? Doesn't he know that the real world is moving too quickly for the youth of today to dwell on the past? The old belief that we study the past in order to make sense of the present and improve the future holds no truth for our student.

Then just when this confident young person believes he is ready to face the challenges of adult life, someone gets the idea that he ought to pass some sort of "cultural literacy" test. Who is Cervantes, Dante, Aristotle, Copernicus? Where is Thailand, Ethiopia, the Nile River—or the capital of his own state? If he could only remember the answers to the questions on that computer trivia game he used to play when he was twelve, maybe he would do all right on the test. Besides, any question he really needs answered can be obtained in a nanosecond on his superpowered, megabyte computer system.

Is he culturally illiterate, or is he just so superior to the generation of his teachers and parents in technology that the same standards cannot be applied to him as were applied to his elders? One cannot help but wonder if he will not feel a twinge of regret when he bounces his own child on his knee at some future date and must plug in the VCR in order to tell a story. Something important is being lost in our lives even though he may not realize it now.

1. Does the essay focus on causes or on effects?

2. What kind of introduction is used? (Review the section on introductions in Chapter Two if necessary.)

3. What is the thesis statement of the essay? Does it make clear the emphasis on cause or effect?

4. Does the author give convincing examples or arguments to support the thesis?

Lowered Standards: Whose Fault?

A popular expression says, "Everybody talks about the problem, but nobody does anything about it." This is certainly true about the state of public education in the United States as we head into the twenty-first century. Parents point the finger at schools; schools blame politicians for failing to allocate adequate funds for education. Politicians speak eloquently about the need for better teachers; teachers decry the lack of parental support. Education specialists design sophisticated tests to assess student achievement and are then devastated when students do not live up to their expectations. Plenty of energy and volumes of hot air are expended in searching for a solution to the problem of students' exiting our public schools without being adequately educated; however, no one has yet looked at those most responsible for the problem: the students themselves.

Let us examine the history of public education in this country. When Horace Mann was putting into practice his idea of a free public education for citizens back in the nineteenth century, he did not express the conviction that air conditioned buildings, swimming pools, comfortable furniture and sophisticated computers were absolute essentials to a sound educational environment. Schools were simple, basic structures. Learning took place because teachers who believed strongly in the value of education dedicated their lives to sharing their knowledge, and students who did not put forth the effort necessary to be promoted were left behind. School work was *work;* school assemblies had not been invented yet, and no one ever took a field trip unless it was planting season and the students were needed on the farms.

Students today are given every possible advantage in the majority of public schools in this country. Money is available for sports teams, landscaped campuses, school dances, and class trips. Children must attend school until they are sixteen years of age whether they deserve to or not. Underachievers are permitted to coast along year after year, absorbing as little as possible of the learning around them and often being passed from one grade to the next due to the sheer exhaustion of the teachers. Making the pep squad or the varsity football team is much more important to many high schoolers than doing well in class. Cheating has become a way of life and even a business for some students. If the students would put half as much effort into studying as they do into finding ways to get around the system, they would graduate from high school much better educated.

Parents can plead, threaten, encourage or punish. Teachers can dream up the most imaginative lesson plans to stimulate learning. Politicians can direct more public funds toward education. Better textbooks and teaching materials can be developed. All of these things are excellent and should be done to the best of the ability of all involved. However, unless students are convinced that education is not merely the steppingstone to a job that will buy them a new Mustang convertible, that it is the foundation of a free society and the right and obligation of all citizens, all the efforts of others will be wasted. Let's stop blaming everybody else for the sorry state of the public school graduate in this country. We know where the responsibility lies: on the shoulders of the pampered, short-sighted students who refuse to see the value of what they are throwing away by resisting education.

1. What type of introduction is used? (Refer to the section on introductions in Chapter Two if necessary.)
2. Is the emphasis on cause or on effect?
3. What is the thesis statement? Does it make clear the emphasis on cause or effect?
4. What kinds of supporting materials are used?
5. Is the author's opinion clear?
6. Is the material adequate to support the author's view?

Indicators of Cause and Effect

Words that are often used to link ideas showing cause and effect fall into six categories with different structures. Notice how an opinion of the author of "A Nation of Illiterates" can be expressed as a cause/effect statement in a variety of ways.

1. The indicator may be the verb phrase in the sentence, with the **cause** in the subject position.

Cause	Indicator	Effect
Too much technology	may lead to can contribute to could result in is one possible reason (for) may be responsible (for)	poor cultural literacy levels.

2. The indicator of cause and effect is the verb phrase in the sentence, with the **effect** in the subject position.

Effect	Indicator	Cause
Poor cultural literacy levels	may come from can stem from could result from may be the result of can be due to are the possible consequences of	too much technology.

3. The indicator is a prepositional phrase.

Indicator	Cause	Effect
Due to Because of	excessive technology,	students often have poor cultural literacy levels.

4. The indicator of cause and effect joins two independent clauses. In this group, notice the punctuation.

Cause	*Indicator*	*Effect*
Many young people have a great deal of technology in their lives;	consequently, therefore, thus, hence	they often have poor cultural literacy levels.
Many young people have a great deal of technology in their lives,	and so so	they often have poor cultural literacy levels.
Many young people have a great deal of technology in their lives.	For this reason, Accordingly,	they often have poor cultural literacy levels.

5. The indicator introduces a subordinate clause joined to a main clause.

Indicator	*Cause*	*Effect*
Since Because	many young people have a great deal of technology in their lives,	they often have poor cultural literacy levels.

These clauses can also be reduced to participial phrases:

> Having a great deal of technology in their lives, many young people today often have poor cultural literacy levels.

6. A conditional structure may be used.

Indicator	*Cause*	*Effect*
If	students have a great deal of technology in their lives,	they may have poor cultural literacy levels.

> If students have a great deal of technology in their lives, they may have poor cultural literacy levels.

Exercise 6. Using Indicators of Cause and Effect

Fill in the blanks with appropriate structures of cause and effect. In some cases, you will have to choose a meaningful verb and use the correct form.

Solar Energy

In the first half of the twentieth century, solar energy was often of interest as a major source of energy, but it was never widely adopted. _____ of underdeveloped technology and manufacturing systems, the competition from the coal, oil, and natural gas industries and later, the competition from the nuclear power industry, the solar energy industry could not compete. In the late 1970s, however, sales of solar water and space heating systems increased greatly. Some of the interest _____ the scarcity of oil and natural gas. Many people were also interested _____ coal is a very dirty fuel. Also, the use of solar energy appeared to be safer than nuclear power; _____, solar energy appeared to be an attractive energy source.

Solar energy was found to have some drawbacks, however. It must be collected and stored in some way. While sunlight is free, technology for storing it is expensive, _____ its use has never been extensive. Studies show that solar heated houses are more economical than electrically heated homes, but the initial cost of installing solar systems is quite high. Oil, gas, and electricity prices rose in the 1980s; _____, there was more demand for solar energy. This increased demand has _____ to increased production, which has lowered prices.

In the late 1980s, oil prices dropped as supplies increased, _____ interest in solar energy waned. Even if solar energy does become more feasible and popular in the future, other problems will arise. Lending banks will need to take into account the high initial cost when lending money to homeowners. Also, buildings using solar energy require access to sunlight. _____, zoning laws will have to be written to prevent buildings from blocking each other's sunlight.

STRUCTURE REVIEW: Using Parallel Structures

One of the cohesive devices writers use to show how parts of a sentence or text are linked together is called *parallelism*. Words, phrases, and clauses that express similar relationships in sentences are expressed in parallel grammatical forms. Compared and contrasted ideas, as well as coordinated ideas in sentences in a paragraph, can also be expressed in parallel forms.

Parallel Word Forms

She is *young, bright,* and *beautiful.* (adjectives)

The speaker spoke *softly* yet *clearly.* (adverbs)

The scientist likes *collecting, organizing,* and *presenting* data. (gerunds)

Parallel Phrases

Because it was late and *(because) we needed a break*, we stopped and closed the restaurant for the night.

The person *who eats too much* and *(who) never exercises* runs the risk of poor health.

*(*Note: the repetition of *because* and *who* is optional.*)*

Parallel Coordinate Conjunctions and Paired Words

not

President Carter, not *President Reagan,* was a peanut farmer.

more...than

He was more *disappointed* than *unhappy* when his colleague was promoted above him.

rather than

Hard work rather than *brilliance* is required for this job.

both...and

He is both a *capable* and a *diligent* worker; he deserves a raise.

not only...but also

Not only *rivers* but also *lakes and oceans* are being polluted by industrial wastes.

whether...or

Whether the *cost of living* rises or the *interest rates* go up, the average citizen does poorly.

neither...nor

Neither the *psychiatrists* nor the *psychologists* have been able to state definitively what causes dreams.

either...or

Either the *president* or the *vice-president* will present the award.

Parallel forms are very important in helping the reader understand the relationship of ideas, and mistakes occur when items that are logically similar are not expressed in parallel forms. For each example of common problems, corrections are given.

Betty likes writing, editing, and to teach.

Betty likes *writing, editing,* and *teaching*. (gerunds)
Betty likes *to write, to edit,* and *to teach*. (infinitives)

My friend is young, a beautiful girl, and artistic.

My friend is *young, beautiful,* and *artistic*. (adjectives)

The teacher taught skillfully and with wit.

The teacher taught *with skill* and *wit*. (nouns)
The teacher taught *skillfully* and *wittily*. (adverbs)

To be a doctor and curing the sick are my goals.

To be a doctor and *cure* the sick are my goals. (infinitives)

Knowing what you want and to do it will bring you success.

Knowing what you want and *doing* it will bring you success. (gerunds)

I'm studying the origin of law and how it developed.

I'm studying the *origin* of law and its *development*. (nouns)
I'm studying how law *originated* and *developed*. (verbs)

Some parallel forms in English are fixed by usage, such as

eyes, ears, and nose
tall, dark, and handsome
soft and cuddly
men, women, and children.

Otherwise, parallel forms can be listed in random order or in some logical order, such as from least to most important, from left to right, from top to bottom, or from youngest to oldest.

We had known Sue as a baby, a child, a teenager, and a young adult.
The roots, trunk, and branches of that tree are infested with insects.

Since parallel forms help convey related meanings, it is important to know how to use them effectively. Not only do parallel forms clarify related ideas, they also simplify writing and make it easier to understand the author's message. Careful use of parallel forms is an important feature of a good writer's style.

Exercise I. Using Parallel Forms

Rewrite the following sentences to correct any errors in parallelism. The first has been done for you.

1. Having no job and poor, the student had to drop out of school.
   Jobless and poor, the student had to drop out of school.
   _____

2. Because he was ill and because of being discouraged, the auto worker left his job.
   _____
   _____

3. A farmer spends his life tilling the soil, sowing the seeds, and he reaps the fruits of his labor.
   _____
   _____

4. The accused man walked slowly and with confidence up to the witness stand.
   _____
   _____

5. Doctors, lawyers, and those who own big businesses make higher salaries than people who work at service jobs.
   _____
   _____

6. While I was in college, I worked as a waitress, as a typist, and I babysat.
   _____
   _____

7. To keep the yard in shape, the bushes should be watered weekly, and you should trim the trees yearly.

   _____

   _____

8. He is a man known for his integrity, and he is honest in business.

   _____

   _____

9. Scientists have been able to pinpoint as well as following the changes that occur during dreams.

   _____

   _____

10. The bones in the body not only give the body shape but also to protect the heart, lungs, brain, etc.

    _____

    _____

Exercise 2. Completing Parallel Forms

Complete the sentences in the following paragraph by filling in the blanks with logical and grammatically correct parallel forms.

Learning a language is a challenging experience, and in order to succeed, a learner must be persistent, unafraid to speak out and _____. As children, we learn our own language without difficulty, but the older we get, the harder a second language is to learn. To understand what we hear, to speak clearly, to read effectively, and _____ correctly takes a long time and a lot of hard work. However, there are several categories of language learners. Because they have a good ear and _____, some people learn a new language very quickly. Others who don't have such a practiced ear or _____ can have a terrible time with language learning. They may take all the right steps, such as spending a lot of time with native speakers, using the language lab, reading as much as possible, and _____, but they still have trouble learning to use the language. Some do very well in listening and speaking but very poorly in _____, while others do very well at writing and very poorly at _____. For these people, learning a language can be a frustrating and _____ experience.

Exercise 3. Writing Parallel Forms

Using the parallel forms suggested, combine each group of sentences. You will have to make some changes in word forms.

Example:

During a deadly fog from December 4 to December 8, in 1952, many Londoners died. Some died because they had hacking coughs. Some had violent nausea. Many found their breath short. (because of + noun)

During a deadly fog from December 4 to December 8 in 1952, many Londoners died because of hacking coughs, violent nausea, and shortness of breath.

1. Billy the Kid was one of the most famous gunfighters in the American "Old West." He was a tall man. He was a slender man. He was a strong man. (adjectives)

   _____

   _____

   _____

2. In 1900, Sigmund Freud published his book, *The Interpretation of Dreams.* He states that dreams are partly about recent experiences. He states that dreams are also about wish fulfillment and long-suppressed desires, fears, and frustrations. (...in which he stated...)

   _____

   _____

   _____

3. Cree is one of the major Canadian Indian languages. It is spoken by 30,000 people. It is written in a system of syllables. (which...)

   _____

   _____

   _____

4. The College of Comedy in Elberon, New Jersey, teaches people to be funny. It is for comedians, gag writers, cartoonists, and other such

professionals. It is for everyone who wants to make laughter a part of everyday life. (not only..., but also...)

_____

_____

_____

5. The area of the Pacific Ocean alone is 25 percent larger than that of all of the land surfaces of the world together. In fact, land is disappearing all of the time. One reason is that land is washed into the sea by rivers. Another reason is that the earth's temperatures are rising and ice caps are melting, causing the water levels of the oceans to rise. (because...) (combine the last three sentences)

_____

_____

_____

6. Elephants are animals of many talents with superior brains and generally docile dispositions. In spite of their massive size, elephants are remarkably agile and light on their feet. In the circus, they do many tricks. They spin balls, walk narrow planks, play catch, stand on their heads, and dance. (such as + gerund) (combine the last two sentences)

_____

_____

_____

7. Peanut butter is a favorite food found in many American pantries because it is inexpensive and nutritious. It is a good source of vitamins, calcium, and iron. Also, peanut butter is an excellent protein supplement. (both as... and as...)

_____

_____

_____

8. Mildred "Babe" Didriksen Zaharias was one of the greatest athletes of all time. In her lifetime, she was able to win 50 major golf tournaments. She set a world record by throwing a baseball 296 feet at a New Jersey AAU meet in 1931. She set the Olympic world record in the javelin throw in 1932. She was able to master tennis, bowling, and basketball easily. (was able to + verb) (combine the last four sentences)

_____

_____

_____

9. Most people think of the panda as a bear, but actually it is related to a raccoon. Like bears, pandas have bad tempers. Like bears, they can use their sharp claws and teeth to show their anger. Like bears, they can be very dangerous. (not only..., but also...) (combine the last three sentences)

   _____

   _____

   _____

10. Several varieties of squash are grown in the United States. The "summer" squashes, including zucchini and pattypan, have soft skins and are quite tender. "Winter" squashes such as hubbard are hard-skinned. (while...) (combine the last two sentences)

    _____

    _____

    _____

Exercise 4. Editing for Parallelism

The following paragraph has some errors due to a lack of parallelism. Find and correct the errors.

Much of New York City's skyline and many of our highest bridges have been built by the Mohawk Indians, natives of New York State. Famed for their ability, indifference to heights, and they can balance well, Mohawks have had positions as riveters on skyscrapers in New York and other North American cities. As early as 1714, an English traveler, John Lawson, observed that a Mohawk could walk on a ridge of a barn of a house and looking down without fear. It was in 1886 that the Mohawks worked on the construction of a bridge spanning the St. Lawrence River. They amazed their employers by running along the half-completed structure, and they ventured into the highest and most dangerous points out of mere curiosity. But they reached the height of their fame as builders and scalers of tall heights during the 1930s in New York City, where they played a major role in the construction of the Empire State Building and Rockefeller Center.

Exercise 5. Correcting Parallelism Errors

Find and correct errors in parallelism.

There are many left-handed people in the United States. Some of them are members of Lefthanders International, an organization that tries to fight discrimination against left-handed people and informing the public about their particular problems. It has been found that more men than women are left-handed and that hand preference doesn't become established until about the age of six.

The left side of the body is controlled by the right side of the brain, which scientists feel is the seat of the emotions, imagination, and where the sense of space is. Many left-handed people learn to drive, sewing, and using machines as well as any right-hander, but it is not easy for them to use many ordinary objects such as tools, gadgets, and knobs usually made for right-handed people. Lefthanders International has been responsible for the opening of many stores that sell special objects such as watches, scissors, pencil sharpeners, and cameras designed especially for left-handed people.

Exercise 6. Sentence Combining Exercise

Before doing this exercise, review the use of parallel forms and structures of coordination and subordination. Combine the sentences with the same numbers. The humor of the conclusion is heightened by the use of parallel constructions.

(1) Betty was lonely. *(1)* She was dateless. *(1)* She felt unhappy. All of her friends had attractive, athletic dates for the Spring Dance. *(2)* Betty thought she was as pretty and as personable as her friends. *(2)* She made a decision to get herself a date. *(3)* She looked in the phone book and called "Perfect Partners." *(3)* "Perfect Partners" was a computer dating service. *(4)* A voice answered and said, "Perfect Partners can give you a better life." *(4)* The voice was soft. *(4)* The voice was sexy. *(4)* The voice had melody.

Betty said that she needed a good date for Saturday night. The voice told her to come to the office to answer some questions and be matched with her perfect partner. *(5)* Betty went to the office where she was given a long form. *(5)* The form contained many questions. *(5)* The questions were about her appearance. *(5)* The questions were about her preferences. *(6)* Betty wrote that she was tall. *(6)* She had blond hair. *(6)* Her face was beautiful. She wrote that her date must be tall, dark, and handsome. Betty went home. *(7)* She waited hopefully. *(7)* She waited with patience.

On Thursday, "Perfect Partners" called and said, "We have your perfect partner. He will arrive at 8:00 on Friday night." On Friday, Betty prepared herself and waited for her date. The doorbell rang at 8:00 sharp. Betty opened the door and gasped. *(8)* A tall, gorgeous man was standing there. *(8)* He looked like a movie star. *(9)* Betty left with him. *(9)* She felt as if she were floating on a cloud. She returned home at midnight, dejected and disappointed. *(10)* She wrote in her diary, "My date was very tall, dark, and handsome, but he was conceited. *(10)* He was a bore. *(10)* He showed stupidity. I'll never trust a machine again!"

WRITING ASSIGNMENT ONE:
Writing About Causes and Effects Together

For this assignment, you are to write an essay with two of your classmates about the major causes or effects of cheating. First, all of you should read the sample newspaper articles that follow. They deal with cases of plagiarism or other forms of academic dishonesty.

Prewriting activity: After reading the following articles, your group should list any *causes* or *effects* of cheating or academic dishonesty, as given in the articles. Also, discuss with your classmates any other possible causes or effects for each instance of cheating and add those to your lists.

Student Denied Diploma Because of Cheating

A student at Central State University who had accumulated all the credits necessary for graduation was denied his diploma when officials discovered that he had cheated on a final exam in his last semester.

An honor review panel of faculty, students, and administrators found John Charles Bullock, a chemistry major, guilty of bringing notes illegally into his final examination in a geology class. The course was an elective and was not required for graduation, but the university ruled that since Bullock had violated school policy by cheating, he was not entitled to receive his degree.

Upon entering college, all students at Central State must sign a pledge stating that they will abide by the university's rules on academic dishonesty. When questioned about his misconduct, Bullock stated that he had been under a great deal of pressure in his senior courses in his major and had not had adequate time to study for his elective course. "I thought that geology would be an easy A," he explained, "but the instructor made us memorize about fifty varieties of rocks. I knew that if I didn't cheat, all the rocks on the final exam would look the same to me." Bullock smuggled into the classroom a chart he had photocopied from one of his textbooks listing characteristics of different rocks. He was caught when his instructor noticed him slipping the rolled chart up his sleeve.

Bullock complained that he had been singled out and made an example of by the university. "Everybody cheats," he stated. "Why didn't the teacher check out the students wearing sunglasses to the exam? All of them had notes pasted inside their lenses. Nobody wants to fail, and it's so easy to get away with cheating in large lecture classes."

Dr. Phillip Stevens, Dean of Students, said that Bullock could return to the university in one year and reapply for admission. His case would be reevaluated then. Stevenson added that it was unlikely that other universities would be willing to accept Bullock because of the black mark on his record. "I had a job waiting for me at Dow Chemical," Bullock said, "but Dow won't hire me now, and my fiancée has called off our wedding. I don't know what I'll be doing in one year. I'm not sure I will ever come back to Central State."

Now discuss with your group the causes and effects of cheating that you found in the article. Why did Bullock cheat in the first place? What effects did his dishonesty have on his life? List the causes and effects below.

Causes (from the article)	Effects (from the article)

Now brainstorm other possible causes and effects of cheating. Can you think of any other reasons why Bullock was dishonest? Can you think of any other effects his cheating may have on his life? List the other possible causes and effects below.

Other possible causes	Other possible effects

Academic Dishonesty Increasing

College and university officials meeting for an annual conference in Anaheim, California, spent the majority of their time dealing with various aspects of academic dishonesty. "We are in a crisis situation," stated Dr. Victor C. Alvarez, president of the American Association of Administrators of Post-Secondary Institutions (AAAPSI). "Never before have students and faculty alike flouted our policies on honesty in such blatant and shameless ways."

When officials compared notes at an opening symposium on "Honesty on Campus," the session had to be extended by two hours to allow time for the relating of many stories of cheating and plagiarism and for discussion of these problems. Among cases cited were the following:

• A professor who plagiarized in three articles he had published and submitted to a tenure committee. The professor tried to justify his action by stating that no one read the articles in professional journals anyway, and that the tenure system forced professors to focus on publication rather than on their primary function, teaching. (The professor was not only denied tenure but dismissed from the university.)

• A student who submitted the same research paper for Sociology II that she had written for Sociology I. "I was busy with my club activities. I didn't think the professors really read the papers, anyway," she said. (The student was given an "F" for the course.)

• A college senior who operated a business buying old research papers and selling them to other students for a profit. He explained that college was expensive and he was trying to help out his parents by paying some of the costs himself. "There are books published on how to cheat in college, with sample term papers and everything," the student complained. "I didn't think I was doing anything illegal. Besides, I only dealt in quality products—papers that had received A or B+ grades. I was offering a valuable service to students who are under pressure to succeed." (This student has been expelled from school and is currently under investigation by the local district attorney's office.)

• A group of foreign students who organized what they called "Study Groups" to help each other get good grades. They wrote papers for each other, shared answers on exams, and even took tests for each other. "The classes are so large that the professors don't know who everyone is, so it was easy," said one group member. "In our culture, it is a terrible loss of face to fail," explained another. "We do not feel we were being dishonest. We were helping each other." (These students were suspended from school and are currently appealing this action.)

AAAPSI officials said that they are working on strategies that will reverse the trend toward increased academic dishonesty. Dr. Alvarez summarized the discussions of the symposium, "Students and teachers alike must be taught that honesty is valued at every institution of higher learning and that cheating will not be tolerated at any level. Faculty members must be given enough flexibility so that their research will not leave them with insufficient time and energy for their teaching duties. International students must learn that we value academic honesty in this culture. All students must come to understand and believe that the learning that takes place on campus is vastly more important than grades earned."

Now discuss with your group the various reasons why people mentioned in the article cheated and the effects academic dishonesty has had on the lives of the people involved. List causes and effects below.

Causes (from the article)	*Effects (from the article)*

Now brainstorm other possible reasons why the people in the article may have cheated and other possible effects their dishonesty may have on their lives. List these possible causes and effects on the following page.

Other possible causes	Other possible effects

Decide on your focus: As a group, discuss whether you want to focus your attention on the causes or effects of academic dishonesty. If you decide to focus on the *causes* of cheating, review the articles for good examples you might include. You can use supporting information from the articles or from your brainstorming discussions on other possible causes. If you decide to focus on the *effects* of cheating on people's lives or on society, you may also refer to the articles and your brainstorming discussions. You will be asked to choose the *three* causes or effects that you think are the most important. Keeping this organization in mind, write a thesis statement that emphasizes what the focus of your essay will be.

Thesis: _____

_____

Plan and outline your essay: Following your discussions with your partners, decide which three causes or effects of cheating you will include in your essay. Write an outline that includes the three major causes or effects you will discuss. Decide what material you will use to support your thesis statement, remembering that you may refer to the articles and/or use your own ideas. Add these details to your outline. You may use the following outline as a guide.

Thesis: _____

_____

I. Cause or effect 1

    A. Supporting idea 1

    B. Supporting idea 2

    C. Supporting idea 3

II. Cause or effect 2

    A. Supporting idea 1

    B. Supporting idea 2

    C. Supporting idea 3

III. Cause or effect 3

    A. Supporting idea 1

    B. Supporting idea 2

    C. Supporting idea 3

Write the introduction with your classmates: Review the types of introductions listed in Chapter Two to decide on an appropriate one.

Write the body of the essay: Each student should take one cause or effect and develop the paragraph related to that one, using the ideas you generated in your group.

Write the conclusion with your classmates: You might want to make a recommendation to students about how to handle situations in which they are tempted—or urged by classmates—to cheat. If you are focusing on effects, your group could decide to write a prediction about what might happen to a person who cheats. Review the section on conclusions in Chapter Three if necessary.

Read and revise the essay: Do this with your peers. Does any part of the essay need to be changed or strengthened? Have you adequately supported your thesis statement?

Edit the essay: Each member of the group should edit the essay for errors in spelling, punctuation, grammar, and sentence structure before the final draft is turned in to the teacher.

WRITING ASSIGNMENT TWO:
Writing About Causes and Effects on Your Own

After a class discussion on one of the following topics, write an essay. Use cause/effect analysis in supporting your topic. As you plan, think about the order of your supporting ideas. As you write, try to use appropriate indicators and transitions between ideas. Share your draft with a partner, asking if the cause/effect relationship is clear and if supporting material is adequate. Edit your draft for spelling, punctuation, grammar, and sentence structure.

Topics:

1. Climate has a great effect on culture, influencing its architecture, the clothes people wear, the vegetation, people's social activities, and so forth. Think of other ways in which climate affects culture. Discuss.

2. Natural disasters, such as hurricanes, floods or fires, and man-made disasters, such as war, can have a devastating effect on a country or an individual. Have you witnessed the effects of any such disaster? Discuss.

3. Many people have a particular skill, talent, ability, or even a handicap that is responsible for the direction their lives take. Discuss some person, perhaps yourself, whose life was affected in one of these ways.

4. Tranquilizers, drugs, alcohol, cigarettes, and all such products result in physical and mental changes in the user. Discuss one or more of these products and the effects on humans.

5. Most historical events have multiple causes. Discuss why a particular historical event occurred.

6. Crime of all kinds is increasing in the United States. Perhaps it is also increasing in other countries. Discuss what may be some of the causes for this increase.

7. Students are under many pressures to succeed and get good grades. Discuss why some students cheat in school as a result.

8. The divorce rate has been increasing. What might be some of the causes for couples' divorcing? Discuss.

SUMMARY WRITING

Part Five: What is a Summary?

As we saw in the first summary-writing lesson, a summary is a short-ened version or condensation of a longer article or text. For students, learning to write summaries is very useful. For one thing, summaries can be used to write down in shortened form what a professor has said in a lecture or what is read in a text. Writing a summary often helps students clarify their own thoughts about a lecture or a reading; likewise, the sum-mary helps students to study for exams, since it is a condensation of the main ideas of the lecture or reading. Some teachers also require students to hand in written summaries of assigned readings or expect students to summarize information to be included in reports or research papers.

In the last four lessons we have been practicing some of the skills needed to write a summary, including finding main ideas and paraphras-ing. In this lesson, we will discuss the form that a summary takes, espe-cially the more formal summary that a teacher might assign.

Of course, the first step in writing an effective summary is to read and understand what is to be summarized. Usually this involves rereading the text several times to get a sense of the author's general thesis and main ideas. After careful reading and outlining (as suggested in the last chapter), you must decide which of the author's ideas are important to include in the summary. After this preparatory work, you will be ready to begin writing your summary.

The first sentence of a summary usually contains a reference to the author and title of the original text if there is one. It also includes the thesis idea. This crucial sentence can take a variety of forms, but for our purposes here it should include *the title, the author* and *the thesis idea.* Here are a few examples of the different forms of first sentences.

1. According to the editor of the *Washington Post,* Thursday, March 20, 1986, Washington, D.C. is running out of space for new memorials. (Here the name of the editor is not known.)

2. M.E. Wallace, in her article, "The Kay-pro Writing Project," reports (states, says, suggests) that incorporating computers into the writing classroom offers many more advantages than disadvantages.

3. The author of "Getting Started on an Exercise Program" in *Today's Health,* December, 1989, suggests (mentions, presents) three impor-tant steps to beginning exercise.

Each of the sentences makes reference to the author and article and also includes the thesis idea. Notice the use of the verbs that are com-monly used in the first sentence of a summary (*reports, suggests*). Other verbs such as *argue, explain* and *describe* may also be used.

Exercise 1. Writing the First Sentence

You are given the name of an author, the name of an article in a magazine or book, and the thesis statement. Work with your classmates and your teacher to write first sentences using the information given. You can use some of the phrases on the previous page in the examples or any other patterns suggested in class.

1. An article from a magazine

Michael Rogers

"Can We Trust Our Software"

Time, January 29, 1990

Thesis: Computers are reliable, but programs that run them can be dangerous and full of problems.

_____

_____

_____

2. A chapter from a book

Leo Buscaglia

Chapter 1, *The Way of the Bull*

Thesis: Life is a trip, a voyage to be enjoyed at all points along the way.

_____

_____

_____

3. A chapter from a book

Kearny, Kearny and Crandall

Chapter 1, *The American Way*

Thesis: The size and ethnic diversity of the United States are very important in defining American life.

_____

_____

_____

4. An article from a magazine

Beryl Benderly

"Everyday Intuition"

Psychology Today, September, 1989

Thesis: Years of learning and repeated challenge can contribute greatly to the development of critical thinking and intuition.

_____

_____

_____

5. An article from a magazine

Paul Kroll

"Is This All There Is?"

The Plain Truth, January, 1990

Thesis: Many have pondered the meaning of life, yet we don't
seem any closer to figuring out this mystery.

_____

_____

_____

Exercise 2. More Practice Paraphrasing

Rewrite each of the following sentences using paraphrasing techniques
that you have learned.

1. Much of New York City's skyline and many of our highest bridges
have been built by the Mohawk Indians, natives of New York State.

_____

_____

_____

2. Famed for their ability, indifference to heights, and balance,
Mohawks have had positions as riveters on skyscrapers in New York
and other North American cities.

_____

_____

_____

3. As early as 1714, an English traveler, John Lawson, observed that a Mohawk could walk on a ridge of a barn or a house and look down without fear.

_____

_____

_____

4. In 1886, while working on the construction of a bridge spanning the St. Lawrence River, the Mohawks amazed their employers by running along the half-completed structure and venturing into the highest and most dangerous points out of mere curiosity.

_____

_____

_____

5. The Mohawks reached the height of their fame as builders and scalers of tall heights during the 1930s in New York City, where they played a major role in the construction of the Empire State Building and Rockefeller Center.

_____

_____

_____

We have worked step by step through the skills necessary for writing a summary: finding main ideas and restating them, paraphrasing, outlining, and writing the introductory sentences for short summaries. In Exercise 5, and also in Chapter 6, as you write some summaries, there are several points to consider. The following checklist will be helpful.

1. The summary begins with the name of the author and the title of the original text as part of the introduction.
2. The main idea of the author is made clear.
3. The main supporting points of the author are stated briefly with unnecessary details omitted and all essential ideas included.
4. The main points are stated objectively without the intrusion of the summary writer's opinions.
5. The author's ideas are paraphrased. If the author is quoted directly, quotation marks are used.

6. The summary is written in clear, logical paragraphs with logical movement from one idea to the next so that a person who has not read the original article can understand clearly the author's ideas.

Writing summaries is not easy, and even native speakers have difficulty deciding how much information to include and how to paraphrase the author's ideas well. Summary writing, however, can become easier with practice.

Exercise 3. Analyzing a Summary

Let's look at a reading and a sample summary. First, read the original essay several times to make sure that you understand each paragraph well. Then fill in the outline. Next, look at the summary. Pay particular attention to the first sentence, which contains the thesis idea and makes reference to the author. The questions at the end of the summary help your analysis.

Earthquake

In 1989, a major earthquake devastated business and residential sections of San Francisco and the surrounding area, destroying a section of the Bay Bridge and an elevated freeway and killing over 75 people. California is earthquake country! The people of the major cities in our state do not ask if there will be another earthquake, they ask when and where it will happen. Although the major earthquakes have been in the San Francisco area so far this century, residents of Los Angeles must ask what the effect on the over 2 million people living in our urban area would be. It is time for the people of Los Angeles to make plans for "the big one."

I.   In the late 1970s, the City Council of Los Angeles made a start by forming an Earthquake Safety Study Committee. The committee found that over 8,000 buildings in the city were unsafe: factories, stores, and dwellings, including apartments and hotels. In the event of an earthquake of 6.0 strength (on the Richter scale of 1.0 to 10.0) there would be an estimated 8,500 deaths and 34,000 injuries. The cost of the damage was estimated at more than $1.2 billion, and it would certainly be much higher today. Most of these buildings would suffer damage because they were built before 1934, when building laws were made stronger. They have weak foundations; the mortar holding the bricks together is not as strong as it used to be; some have suffered from earlier quakes. The committee concluded that conditions were not very good, and little improvement has been made.

II. However, there is a cure. Most of these buildings can be reinforced, made safer by adding steel rods and by making the foundations stronger. Many owners of dangerous buildings have already made these improvements. It is hard to be accurate, but the cost has been between $6 and $10 per square foot. At an average cost of, say, $8 per square foot, it would take a total of $700 million to make downtown Los Angeles safer.

III. Property owners, insurance people, and other citizens have asked, "Where is the money going to come from?" The federal government will give disaster loans, but only after the destruction. Are the owners supposed to bear the cost? Will they raise the rents to make up the expense? Will banks lend the money at low interest rates? At what point will an owner say that it is too costly to fix his building and just walk away? Is it really the business of the city council to pass a law requiring all buildings to be made safer?

Many of these questions and objections are honest, but the people who ask them miss the main point: What will be the cost if nothing is done? Is the loss of property and human lives worth less than the cost of reinforcement? Clearly, it is the duty of the city council to the citizens to protect them by passing earthquake laws and making Los Angeles a safer place to live.

Tom Smith

Thesis: _____

_____

  I. (Main idea) _____

_____

 II. (Main idea) _____

_____

III. (Main idea) _____

_____

Summary

Tom Smith, the author of "Earthquake," feels strongly that the people of Los Angeles should make preparations for the consequences of a major earthquake. The Los Angeles City Council found that over 8,000 buildings in the city were unsafe, and that in the event of an earthquake, the loss of life and property would be enormous. Although most of the unsafe buildings can be reinforced, it is estimated that it would cost at least $700 million to make the city safer. Many people ask where this money should come from—individual owners, the federal government, the city itself? The author feels that no matter what the questions or objections may be, it is up to the City Council to protect the citizens and make them as safe from earthquakes as possible.

1. Does the summary contain these points?

_____ The summary begins with the name of the author and the title of the original text.

_____ The main idea of the article is clear.

_____ The author's main supporting points are stated briefly with unnecessary details omitted.

_____ The main points are stated objectively.

_____ The author's ideas are paraphrased or quotation marks are used.

_____ Clear paragraph style is used for the summary.

2. Does the author of the summary include the same main ideas that you had in your outline?

Exercise 4. Analyzing a Summary

Follow the directions for Exercise 3 as you analyze another summary.

Student Rights

Who knows better than the students themselves what a university should do for them and how they should be treated? Yet how often do students have any say at all in such important issues as faculty selection, curriculum planning, and scheduling? The answer is obvious: never. If university administrations refuse to include student representatives in the decision-making process, something drastic must be done.

I.   Let's examine what is happening right here on our own campus in the areas mentioned above. The first major issue is the selection of faculty members. Never in the history of this college has a student been permitted to interview, examine the credential of, or even meet prospective professors. All hiring is done by a joint administrative-faculty committee, often made up of people who will not even have extensive dealings with the individuals after they begin teaching. Those who have the most at stake and whose lives and academic careers will be governed by the professors—the students themselves—never even meet the new teachers until the first class meeting. No one is better equipped to evaluate a professor's ability to communicate with students than those whom he or she intends to teach. Anyone can read a curriculum vitae to ascertain the level of professional training and experience someone has had, but the best judges of a teacher's ability to teach, which is the primary function of any professor, are undoubtedly the students themselves.

II.   Students' interest in and commitment to appropriate curricula are even more obvious. We have come to college with very specific purposes in mind: to prepare ourselves intellectually and practically for the future. We know what we need to learn in order to compete successfully with others in our chosen fields. Why should we be kept out of the curriculum planning process? If we pay for the textbooks, spend hours in the library doing research, and burn the midnight oil studying for tests and exams, why are we not permitted to give our opinions about the materials we will spend so many hours studying? It is imperative that our views be made known to curriculum planners.

III.   Finally, the area of scheduling is of vital interest to students. The hours at which classes are offered affect us daily. Many of us must juggle work and class schedules, but often administrators ignore such problems when they schedule classes. Schedules must be convenient and flexible so that all students have equal opportunities to take the most popular classes and those that are most essential to their majors. If students helped with scheduling, never would there be two required courses offered at the same time for only one semester per academic year. Never would we have to wait two or three semesters to take a course that is a prerequisite for other desired courses, nor would we have to race across campus in ten minutes to get from one class to the next. Students are vitally concerned with scheduling.

In the 1960s and early 1970s, students were not too shy or fearful to demonstrate against the injustices they saw in the draft system and the Vietnam conflict. Why should students today be afraid to voice their opinions about the very important issues that affect their lives? It is imperative that students act to protect their rights. Fellow university students, I urge that you meet together and draw up demands to be presented to the administration. We must take the future in our own hands, not be led to it like passive sheep. Let us act now so that we will not be sorry later.

Jeff Bakersfield

Thesis: _____

_____

I. (Main idea) _____

_____

II. (Main idea) _____

_____

III. (Main idea) _____

_____

Summary

In his essay, "Student Rights," Jeff Bakersfield, a university student, states that students have the right to be involved in university administrative decisions. Using the current situation on his own college campus as an example, he emphasizes that students should be included in decisions regarding selection of faculty, curriculum planning, and scheduling of classes. He points out that students not only have more vital interests in the decisions made in these areas than those who traditionally settle the issues, but that they are also better equipped through their experiences as students to make intelligent decisions about them. Bakersfield concludes by stating that it is crucial for students to become actively involved in protesting unilateral administrative decisions and proposes that they meet to discuss their mutual interests and demands.

1. Does the summary contain the following points?

_____ The summary begins with the name of the author and the title of the original text.

_____ The author's thesis statement is clear.

_____ The author's main supporting points are stated briefly with unnecessary details omitted.

_____ The main points are stated objectively.

_____ The author's ideas are paraphrased or quotation marks are used.

_____ Clear paragraph style is used for the summary.

2. Does the summary contain the main ideas that you included in your outline?

Exercise 5. Writing a Summary

A good technique for training yourself in summary writing skills is to read an original piece of writing and then close the book. Write down the author's ideas in your own words without referring to the original. Then go back to the original writing and check your summary for accuracy and objectivity.

Using this technique, write a brief summary of an editorial or essay you find in a newspaper. Use paraphrasing techniques that you have been practicing.

(Note to the teacher: You may suggest local newspapers or national magazines or newspapers in which your students will find essays of appropriate complexity and length.)

Chapter Six
Focus on Content: Using Argumentation

WRITING AN ARGUMENTATIVE ESSAY

You have learned a variety of ways to organize essays and have practiced ways to communicate ideas effectively. Now you are going to use this learning to persuade. When your purpose is to persuade a reader that your opinion is valid or to change a reader's mind about a particular subject, you write an *argumentative* essay.

Argumentation reflects a *purpose* for writing. People use argumentation frequently in everyday conversations. For example, you may want to persuade a friend not to drive after drinking too much alcohol at a party. You use all the logical arguments you can think of to get him or her to give up the car keys. You may even cite statistics about the number of alcohol-related accidents. If your friend offers a counter-argument, such as a claim that he or she is sober enough to drive, you will refute it as strongly as possible, perhaps by asking for proof of sobriety. You might ask your friend to walk a straight line or recite a well-known nursery rhyme. In summary, you will do your best to convince your friend because you believe you are right.

Writing an argumentation essay is a similar process. First, you must decide how you feel about a particular issue. If your opinion is not clearly defined in your own mind, you will never be able to persuade someone else of its validity. The introductory paragraph of your essay will include a *thesis statement* that does two things: (1) defines the issue and (2) presents your opinion of it. In developing your thesis, consider your audience. To whom are you writing? How much proof will be necessary to convince the reader?

In fact, some readers may never be convinced about a particular issue, no matter how strong your support is, because of deeply held personal beliefs. The expression "Never argue about religion or politics" could be extended to other issues. Argumentation is effective only when ideas can be presented (and subsequently accepted or rejected) logically. One cannot logically debate religious beliefs, facts, or individual taste. For example, you may believe that blue is the most beautiful color in the world, but you will never persuade someone who prefers red. Likewise, it is ridiculous to argue about a fact (such as who won the World Cup in a particular year) because simple research will answer the question.

Also, be sure your argument is supported by logic rather than emotion. Observe how the writer makes an emotional appeal to convince the reader in the following sentences.

1. Ruth is the most beautiful name in the English language because that is the name of the sweetest, kindest woman in the world: my mother.

2. Voting for John P. Politician for mayor would be comparable to casting your ballot for Mussolini!

3. How could anyone look into the eyes of an adorable, innocent little kitten and defend the right of local animal shelters to kill unwanted pets?

4. Drug dealers should receive the death penalty because the drugs they sell could fall into the hands of your own children and ruin their lives.

In each of these sentences, the support for the writer's opinion is based solely on emotions, with no regard for logical proof.

Exercise 1. Determining Logical Opinions

Test your understanding of the types of opinions that may be argued logically by reading the following sentences and putting a check mark by those that can be debated.

_____   1. All handguns should be banned by law.

_____   2. The study of music is an important part of a liberal education.

_____   3. The Metropolitan Opera presented five concerts in Cleveland during the winter of 1990.

_____   4. Honesty is the best policy.

_____   5. Only bonafide members of the Republican Party know how to solve the economic crisis.

_____   6. Renaissance art is more beautiful than Baroque art.

_____   7. Children of illegal refugee aliens should be denied free public education.

_____   8. A day will come when all sinners will be judged.

_____   9. Our parklands must be saved from destruction by greedy land developers.

_____   10. The government should provide free day care services for working mothers.

Consider why you rejected any of the above statements. Were they statements of fact? Were they based on emotional or illogical appeals?

Now look at the statements you selected as debatable. How many included a modal auxiliary verb? It is likely that a statement of opinion will make use of a modal that shows *advisability* (*should, ought to*) or *strong necessity* (*must, have to, had better*). These modals show that the writer is trying to influence the reader or get him to modify his behavior in some way. The use of more tentative modals such as *may, might,* or *could* (for *possibility*) can weaken the opinion statements. Which of the following offers the strongest opinion?

1. It might be a good idea for citizens to plant home gardens in order to make efficient use of our natural resources.
2. Citizens had better begin to make efficient use of our natural resources by planting home gardens.
3. Every citizen should consider planting a home garden in order to make efficient use of our natural resources.

As you read the opinions in Exercise 1 you may have realized that there can be more than two sides to an issue. In a debate, only two choices are given. For example, in the sentence "All handguns should be banned by law," you must either agree or disagree with the opinion. Either handguns should be forbidden or they should not. This is sometimes called a pro (for) or con (against) argument. In response to "Children of illegal refugee aliens should be denied free public education," you might think of several viewpoints, such as the following:

1. Children are the innocent victims of their parents' unlawful immigration; therefore, they should not be punished.
2. Illegal immigrants do not pay taxes or support public schools; their children should not be allowed to attend public schools.
3. The children will become even more expensive to society if they are allowed to grow up uneducated; a tuition-scholarship program should be developed to support the education of these children.

Argumentation with multiple choices usually occurs when a problem is presented. Various points of view will arise as people try to come up with solutions to the problem. Remember, however, that once you have decided on your own viewpoint, all your supporting arguments must be designed to convince a reader of that opinion.

In the essay that follows, the author expresses a particular opinion. Read it and answer the questions that follow:

Education Benefits for Illegals?

When will the United States learn that it cannot ignore law in attempting to solve the problems of the whole world? It is certainly unfortunate that some of our Latin American neighbors are struggling with astronomical inflation rates and extremely high levels of unemployment causing a high level of emigration by people seeking better economic conditions. I certainly count myself among the strongest supporters of foreign aid for such unhappy nations. However, I insist that all efforts to help the people of these nations be made lawfully. In the case of illegal immigrants, no special exceptions should be made, even if this means denying free education to their children.

No one knows for certain how many illegal immigrants today reside in our country, competing for jobs, housing, and social services with our legal residents. Even recent legislation designed to deal with this problem has not kept certain areas of our nation, notably Texas and other southwestern states, from being overburdened by this situation. When the innocent young children of these immigrants flood the schools, they place special economic (as well as educational and psychological) demands upon the local school systems. Are we morally, if not legally, obligated to provide free education to these children? I say no! For three compelling reasons, accepting these children into our public schools is wrong.

First, it places an undue economic hardship on the local school districts. What other district in the affected state would be willing to share the cost in terms of tax dollars? For instance, if the city of Houston, Texas, spent an average of $500,000 per year to educate illegal immigrants, would Dallas be required to pay a percentage of the bill? Must the states of Oklahoma, Arkansas, and Arizona chip in a share also? How about distant states such as Maine and Alaska, which do not even have an immigrant problem—must they be asked to bear the burden, too? On the other hand, Texans will argue, quite justifiably, that the problem is one of national, not regional, implications. It is unfair to expect certain states or districts, simply due to geographic location (nearness to borders), to accept all responsibility for the education of these children.

Second, the permission of such free education encourages, rather than discourages, illegal immigration. Not only will prospective refugees dream of relatively high-paying jobs and better living standards, but they will expect our society to provide their children with all the benefits of an American public-school education. What a temptation to even the most law-abiding resident of an oppressed nation!

Finally, the whole situation encourages the belief by the general public that breaking the law is all right as long as the reason is a good moral one. This leads to the dangerous conclusion that "the end justifies the means." Isn't this the way Hitler attempted to justify his atrocities? Do we wish to fall into the same trap?

Therefore, I call upon our legislators to act swiftly in passing strong legislation outlawing the admission of illegals into our public schools. We must not forget that we were **all** once immigrants who entered this country lawfully and became law-abiding citizens. Obedience to the law is an important reason why we are a strong nation. If we let our laws be broken for reasons that some consider justified, how will we be able to defend all other laws?

Ralph P. Anderson

Now answer these questions:

1. What is the problem suggested by Mr. Anderson?
2. What is the author's opinion, according to the thesis statement?
3. No matter what your opinion of the problem is, does the author give strong support for his opinions? What are his supporting arguments?
4. Does he use any supporting material that appeals to emotions rather than logic?
5. Which modals and conditional structures are used? What is their function?
6. What is the author's conclusion?

Providing Support for an Argument

Because you know that your reader may not be easily convinced, you need to be especially careful as you develop the supporting arguments for this type of essay. For this reason, keep these points in mind.

Be prepared to refute another person's argument. This means that you have already read or heard an opposing point of view, and the purpose of your essay is to offer counterarguments to it. In order to refute another's arguments effectively, you may need to research the topic and obtain facts and statistics that support your counter view.

Be careful to use appropriate and accurate statistics in your support. Examine these statements:

> Children who use fluoride toothpaste get 72 percent fewer cavities than those who do not. Therefore, all children should use fluoride toothpaste.

Now ask yourself these questions:

> Where did the "72 percent" figure come from? Was it a reliable source, such as a recent, statistically sound survey?
>
> Is the figure accurate? Can you verify it by checking the source?
>
> Are the statistics appropriate? Does it follow logically that all children should use a fluoride toothpaste?

Good statistical support of argumentative statements involves both accurate and appropriate facts that lead directly to the conclusion the writer wishes to convey.

Be thorough and avoid oversimplification. This means that sufficient choices must be given as solutions to problems that may be attacked in more than one way. Can you offer other possible solutions to the problems mentioned in the following statements?

The only way to lose weight is to exercise.

If you want a good job, you must study at a well-known university.

You should choose a college by examining its convenience to the subway or bus system.

Certainly, you must have thought of other ways to lose weight (eat low-calorie or low-fat food, eat less), get a good job (go to a technical school, apply to many places, use your friends and acquaintances as contacts), and choose a college (ask friends' advice, seek academic counseling, look at programs offered, look for respected faculty). By offering only one choice to a solution, you open yourself to attack by opponents of your viewpoint. Anticipate what your opponents may criticize in your essay. Ward off these attacks by not oversimplifying the choices you offer and by refuting possible opposition.

Make sure that any cause/effect relationship you mention is correct and logical. Because one event precedes another chronologically does not necessarily mean that the first event resulted in the second. Observe the faulty cause/effect conclusions in the following examples.

After Ricardo quit smoking, he got lots of colds. Conclusion: Smoking prevents colds.

Mary Smith crossed her fingers right before her job interview, and she got the job. Conclusion: crossing her fingers assured her of getting the job.

It should be obvious that these sequential events represent nothing more than coincidences, not causal relationships.

Exercise 2. Supporting and Refuting an Argument

Work with a partner to do this exercise. For each thesis statement that follows, each of you separately is to write down as many supporting reasons as you can think of, avoiding emotional or illogical arguments, oversimplification, or faulty cause/effect conclusions. Then exchange lists and try to refute each of your partner's supporting ideas. When you have finished, compare your results with your partner's. Was either of you unable to refute any of the arguments? Those are probably the strongest supporting statements. Make a combined list of all the strongest arguments that you and your partner developed. Save the list for a future writing assignment.

1. Smoking should be banned in all public places.

   Supporting statements

   _____

   _____

   _____

   Statements that refute the above arguments

   _____

   _____

   _____

2. Animals should not be used in medical research.

   Supporting statements

   _____

   _____

   _____

   Statements that refute the above arguments

   _____

   _____

   _____

3. Private schools should receive federal and state tax money.

   Supporting statements

   _____

   _____

   _____

   Statements that refute the above arguments

   _____

   _____

   _____

Debating Opinions Informally—A Cooperative Prewriting Activity

A debate is a structured discussion of opposing opinions. You will practice an informal debate to prepare for writing argumentative essays later.

The teacher will divide you into an even number of small groups. Each pair of groups will then be assigned one of the argumentative topics that follow this discussion, with each group defending an opposing viewpoint. For example, two groups could be assigned the topic "Capital punishment should be allowed." One group would take the "affirmative" position (*for* the statement) and the other the "negative" viewpoint (*against* the statement).

Each group must come up with a list of convincing arguments to support its stand. Even if you are assigned to a group that is defending a viewpoint you do not personally hold, try to think of supporting arguments. Make a list in writing and organize it in any appropriate way (from least to most important, from least to most familiar details, and so on). Then try to anticipate what the opposing group will say to support its point of view. Write down counterarguments to all the points you believe the other group will present.

Next, debate the issue informally in class. You might arrange your chairs in two rows opposite each other in the front of the class. The teacher will act as the moderator and will give each side equal time to present its viewpoint and refute the other's. You can choose one person to be the spokesperson to present your group's arguments and another person to refute the other side's statements, or you may each take a turn presenting some of the argument.

At the conclusion of each debate, you should vote on which side won. The winner should be determined not on the basis of the personal opinions of the members of the class regarding the topic, but rather on the basis of the quality of the supporting arguments for each side and the effectiveness of the presentations. Topics may be assigned from the following list.

1. Final exams should be used as the only measure to determine a student's final grade.
2. Capital punishment should be allowed.
3. There should be an international law permitting nations with seacoasts to claim a certain amount of the coastal ocean (say five or ten miles or more) as their own territory.
4. Industries that pollute the air or water around them should be solely responsible for cleaning up the pollution they have caused.
5. All parking on publicly owned streets should be free.
6. Olympic athletes should be allowed to accept money for their participation in sports events.
7. Scientists, not the government, should determine when human life begins and ends.
8. Computer "hackers" (people who learn how to tap into private information systems on their home computers) should be prosecuted as common criminals.

9. Individuals have the right to educate their children at home rather than in schools.

10. The civil laws of a nation should have priority over the religious beliefs of individual groups.

STRUCTURE REVIEW: Sentence Errors

Sentence Fragments

A fragment is a piece broken off from some whole, such as a fragment of glass. A sentence fragment is, therefore, a piece of a sentence. Fragments can occur when adjective clauses or adverbial clauses are not attached to independent clauses and are punctuated as separate sentences. Adjective and adverbial clauses are dependent clauses and cannot stand alone. Fragments can also occur for some other reasons. Professional writers often use fragments for effect (surprise, emphasis, etc.), but in general, it is best not to use sentence fragments in academic writing.

Look at the examples of sentence fragments (in *italics*) below:

Adverbial clause fragment

We missed the bus this morning.
Because our alarm didn't go off.

Adjective clause fragment

You may give the message to anyone.
Who answers the phone.

Appositive fragment

Our new neighbors are the Trans.
Refugees from Vietnam.

Participial fragment

The young worker was struck by a car.
Riding a bicycle to his job.

Noun clause fragment

The newspaper reported that there was an earthquake in Japan.
Also that many people were injured.

Compound verbs

The dance began at 8:00.

And lasted until midnight.

Examples and details

John likes many sports.

Such as tennis, basketball, and table tennis.

Note on introducing examples: The words *for instance, for example,* and *also* may begin new sentences, but the words *such as* and *especially* may not. Examples:

Juan is a very good writer and has even won awards. *For instance,* just last year he was awarded $100 for his essay on patriotism in America.

High school students who take advanced mathematics classes, *such as* trigonometry and calculus, usually score higher on college entrance math exams than those who take only algebra or geometry.

Exercise I. Identifying Sentence Fragments

In the space to the left of each number, write an *S* if the string of words is a complete sentence or an *F* if it is a fragment of a sentence. Can you identify the cause of the fragment? The first two are done for you.

_____*S*_____ 1. Tom's parents are planning to leave for Europe in May.

_____*F*_____ 2. Although the snow has melted.

_____ 3. For example, our firm delivers furniture free of charge.

_____ 4. Because they had studied hard, they found the test easy.

_____ 5. Especially the high cost of living.

_____ 6. Since David wanted a snack, he went into the kitchen.

_____ 7. Whenever she looked out the window.

_____ 8. And that flowers were in bloom.

_____ 9. Beaten at their own game.

_____ 10. Following the president's lead, all members sat down.

_____ 11. The writer who was known for her radical ideas.

_____ 12. Whose home is on the Mexican border.

_____ 13. Parents who can attend the meeting.

_____ 14. Also, the wives and children of the players.

_____ 15. Everyone is welcome.

There are two ways to correct sentence fragments, one of which is simply to correct the punctuation. To do this, you must identify the independent clause to which the fragment belongs and attach it, using appropriate punctuation. Note the following error and correction:

Fragment

It is important to eat leafy green vegetables. Such as spinach and kale.

Correction

It is important to eat leafy green vegetables, such as spinach and kale.

Sometimes you need to change the sentence structure if you cannot identify an independent clause to which the fragment should be attached:

Misuse of participle

Before winning an Oscar, the actor _known_ as one of the most talented people in his profession.

Corrected by completing the verb phrase

Before winning an Oscar, the actor _was known_ as one of the most talented people in his profession.

No subject

If you want to write correct English sentences, is necessary to edit your work for sentence fragments.

Corrected by adding the subject

If you want to write correct English sentences, _it_ is necessary to edit your work for sentence fragments.

You may need to delete a conjunction that is not appropriate or change a participial phrase to an independent clause:

Inappropriate subordinating conjunction

The Browns really wanted to buy a new home in an exclusive section of town; however, they couldn't afford it. _Although_ they didn't have incomes that were high enough.

Corrected by deleting the conjunction

The Browns really wanted to buy a new home in an exclusive section of town; however, they couldn't afford it. They didn't have incomes that were high enough.

Corrected by changing the conjunction

The Browns really wanted to buy a new home in an exclusive section of town; however, they couldn't afford it *because* they didn't have incomes that were high enough.

Participial phrase used

While listening to the long, boring lecture by the students' substitute economics professor.

Corrected by rewriting

The students listened to the long, boring lecture by their substitute economics professor.

Exercise 2. Correcting Sentence Fragments

Correct the following sentence fragments in any appropriate way. The first has been done for you.

1. Iran, located in Southwest Asia, stretching from the Caspian Sea to the Arabian Sea.

   Iran, located in Southwest Asia, stretches from the Caspian Sea to the Arabian Sea.

   _____

2. On the west, it is bordered by Iraq and Turkey. And on the north by the Caspian Sea and the Soviet Union.

   _____

   _____

3. While Oman lies to the south. Pakistan and Afghanistan border it on the east.

   _____

   _____

4. The total area of Iran is 1,648,000 square kilometers. Which is a bit larger that the area of the state of Alaska.

   _____

   _____

5. The population is mixed. Composed of Indo-Europeans, Turks, Kurds, Lur, Semitic Arabs, and others.

   _____

   _____

6. Islam, the religious preference of most Iranians.

_____

_____

7. Without oil, the most important product in its economy, would never have been able to progress as it has since 1960.

_____

_____

8. Second only to Saudi Arabia in oil production in the Persian Gulf.

_____

_____

Exercise 3. Editing for Sentence Fragments

Identify and correct any sentence fragments in the following paragraph.

Sound is the result of vibration. Which is simply the moving back and forth of some object. However, in order for these vibrations to be heard. They must take place in some medium, something to carry the sound from its source to the hearer. For instance, air, a liquid or a solid. When the vibration is very regular. The result is a musical sound. If the vibration is not regular, the effect on your ears is not pleasing. The resulting sound is called "noise."

Run-on Sentences

Run-on sentences are two or more independent clauses that have been joined inappropriately. (For appropriate sentence connectors and punctuation for coordination, review the charts on coordination and punctuation in Appendix 2.) The following is correct coordination:

It's too cold to walk to school; moreover, it's too far.

Without a connecting word, merely a comma, or a sentence connector punctuated incorrectly, you would have a run-on sentence, such as in the following incorrect examples:

No punctuation

It's too cold to walk to school it's too far.

Comma used incorrectly

It's too cold to walk to school, it's too far.

Connector not punctuated correctly

It's too cold to walk to school, in addition, it's too far.

Often a run-on sentence is caused by a modifying phrase that could be at the end of one sentence or at the beginning of the next:

Meteorologists can track hurricanes *when they are predicted,* citizens can take appropriate precautions.

To correct the run-on sentence, you must decide which independent clause to attach the "when" time clause to and break the sentence at the appropriate point:

Meteorologists can track hurricanes. *When they are predicted*, citizens can take appropriate precautions.

Sometimes the second independent clause begins with a pronoun, and the writer may not recognize the pronoun as the subject of a new independent clause:

Identical twins tend to be extremely sensitive to each other, one often anticipates the feelings of the other.

To correct this sentence, you may change the comma to a period or a semicolon:

Identical twins tend to be extremely sensitive to each other. One often anticipates the feelings of the other.

Identical twins tend to be extremely sensitive to each other; one often anticipates the feelings of the other.

Another way to correct this run-on sentence is to add a conjunction or a sentence connector:

Identical twins tend to be extremely sensitive to each other. *In fact,* one often anticipates the feelings of the other.

Exercise 4. Identifying Run-on Sentences

The following are run-on sentences. For each independent clause, underline the subject once and the verb twice. Draw a line between the clauses. The first has been done for you.

1. <u>Mandarin Chinese</u> is <u>spoken</u> by more speakers than any other language,/<u>it</u> <u>is</u> one of the world's oldest *tongues*.

2. Mandarin Chinese is spoken on mainland China and Taiwan it is spoken by almost 700 million people.

3. It became China's official language in 1644 the Manchu overthrew the Ming dynasty at that time.

4. The new rulers spoke many languages they chose Peking Mandarin to be the political language.

5. Later, its use spread it was chosen as the country's official language.

6. Many characters are used to write Mandarin, however, they bear no relation to the words' sounds.

7. Early Chinese characters were like pictures now they are more abstract.

8. There are about 50,000 Chinese characters, a ten-year-old child knows about 200.

9. Mandarin is a tone language it has four tones; moreover, some dialects have nine tones.

10. So many people speak Chinese, many Americans want to learn it.

Exercise 5. Rewriting Run-on Sentences

Rewrite any sentences that contain run-ons. Use connecting words, where possible. (Some sentences may be correct; if so, write *correct.*) The first has been done for you.

1. Marijuana is dangerous because it's a narcotic-type drug some people may smoke it while they are driving.

   Marijuana is dangerous because it's a narcotic-type drug; nevertheless, some people smoke it while they are driving.

2. We ran out of gas and had a flat tire, the journey took us all day.

   _____

   _____

3. Exploring outer space is the last adventure of modern man, it matches the excitement of the exploration of the New World.

   _____

   _____

4. My sister considers herself liberated, but she has decided to be a housewife.

   _____

   _____

5. I applied for a job as a nurse's aide since I love helping people I hope I get it.

_____

_____

6. The candidate enjoys wide support from the voters because of his record he will probably be elected.

_____

_____

7. The actor refused to accept a role as a gangster because he wanted to protect his image, he was famous for his hero roles.

_____

_____

8. When my birthday comes, I invite my friends over to my house to celebrate, this gives us a chance to see each other again.

_____

_____

9. Children hate to go to bed early because they don't want to miss anything, so they use various strategies to delay the bedtime hour.

_____

_____

10. Every gun in the United States should be registered it is safer for all people and it is good for the security of the public.

_____

_____

Exercise 6. Editing for Run-on Sentences

Find and correct any errors in run-on sentences.

Paragraph 1:

Depending on credit cards for all your purchases can be a dangerous practice. It is very convenient to carry just one little piece of plastic instead of a lot of money when you go shopping, it is also safer than carrying cash. However, when that big bill comes at the end of the month, careless shoppers might be in for a very unpleasant surprise, then they often pay only the minimum amount due, and they are charged very high interest rates for the balance. If the shoppers charge more purchases during the next month, their next monthly bill will be even higher, the situation is now becoming very serious. Some shoppers get so deeply into debt that it takes them months or even years to get out. "Plastic money" can be very useful for taking advantage of unexpected sales or bailing people out in emergencies, but it must be handled wisely, then shoppers will have the convenience but none of the dangers of having credit.

Paragraph 2:

Experts in child-rearing agree that children need a lot of affection, however, they also need discipline. Although many parents realize that their sons and daughters require love and care, they neglect to provide supervision. Their children are allowed to act as they wish, in short, they are completely uncontrolled. Every parent has the responsibility of teaching moral values, nevertheless, parents have often been reluctant to exercise authority. They believe that strictness will cause their children not to love them it has been proven that children who receive both love and discipline are happier, better adjusted, and also more self-confident.

USING SUMMARY WRITING IN ARGUMENTATION

Writing argumentative essays involves preparing logical arguments and often refuting another's ideas. In order to do this, summarizing is often necessary. The summary can then be supported or refuted by the author, according to his or her own viewpoint. Remember these steps in writing good summaries:

1. *Cite your source.* In this way, you attribute the opinion you are summarizing to the appropriate person(s). As was explained in the discussion of appropriate support for argumentative essays, it is often important to know how reliable the original writer is.

2. *Present the author's controlling idea.* A summary gives the author's purpose and thesis at the very outset. The topic of the original work should be clear from the beginning of the summary.

3. *Clarify the author's attitude.* This is especially important in argumentative writing. Remember that the summary is not the place to present an opposing viewpoint. You may do this after clarifying the original point of view in the summary.

4. *Include supporting examples or details.* Sometimes the purpose of summarizing is to agree with the author's viewpoint and to write an argumentative essay that strengthens or extends the original author's ideas. In this case, including summarized details and examples could be quite effective.

In a summary, you may present your own opinion of the author's ideas in subsequent parts of the essay, but not in the summary itself. Think of a summary as a kind of first-page newspaper report. Journalists are expected to present the news objectively on the first page, with their personal opinions reserved for the editorial section. A summary must be like that; you will have your chance to editorialize later.

Exercise 1. Summarizing for Argumentation 1

Read the following essay about future technological developments in traffic control. Write a summary of the article. Then write your opinion of this future system in another paragraph. Do you think it is a good idea for our traffic to be computer-controlled without direct input from the drivers?

Smart Roads of the Future

Your car enters the on-ramp, ready to enter into the southbound traffic stream. The car speaker beeps three times telling you that a sensor in the highway asphalt has recorded your car's ID number. Your car is now controlled by the highway navigation system.

You take your foot off the gas, open the newspaper and start to read. As a space opens in the lane next to you, your car moves to the opening. Front and rear radar-controlled autopilots adjust the distance between the vehicles. As you pass a toll booth, a detector reads a radio signal from your license plates and debits your credit card for the toll. Another sensor lets you know about an accident up ahead so you can change your travel route.

Does this sound like some space-age dream? Surprise! Some of this technology is already in place and more is on the way. In the U.S., millions of dollars of federal funds are being allocated to build an Intelligent Vehicle-Highway System (IVHS) better known as the "smart" highway. Such a system will save billions of dollars in lost worker productivity due to highway congestion by reducing the average commute by 50%. It will also reduce air pollution, reduce the number of traffic accidents, and reduce stress in the driving population.

Developing the IVHS will take place in three stages. The first stage will be to develop management systems to collect data on highway conditions. Next will be traveler-advice devices to transmit information to the car. Finally will be the systems to automatically control the speed, direction, steering and braking of the car.

Surprisingly, the first two systems are already in place in many areas, including Europe, Japan, and the U.S. In Germany and England for example, infrared beams now shoot information from roadside stations to cars as they pass by. Other systems are being tested that will enable drivers to pick up information from a band of an existing FM radio station or from a UHF radio signal. They are designed to provide travel information that can be shown on electronic software maps inside of vehicles.

In the U.S., a congested Virginia highway leading into Washington, D.C. is implanted with six-foot loops of wire through which an electric current passes to create a magnetic field. A car passing over the field causes the current in the wire to change frequency. The change is recorded by roadside data collecting equipment and the results are sent to a computer. The computer instructs traffic lights at on-ramps to delay traffic entering the highway. An estimated 6% of big city interstates in the U.S. have such sensors. In other states, systems are being tested to provide drivers with maps of cities, restaurant and hotel information, and ideal travel routes.

The third stage of development of the "smart" highway is still many years in the future. Although the University of California at Berkeley is presently studying a remote guidance system that will allow cars to follow a painted stripe on a highway, the ultimate system still faces many obstacles. All indications are, however, that we can look forward to a time when we will get in our cars and settle back with our paper and coffee, leaving the driving up to the highway and the car. The future may not be so far away!

Adapted from "Robo-Roads: Making Highways Smart"
by Curt Suplee, *The Washington Post,*
May 27, 1991

Exercise 2. Summarizing for Argumentation   II

Read the two "letters to the editor" that follow. Each letter is an argumentative essay expressing a different viewpoint about women's roles in contemporary society. Summarize the opposing viewpoints, using your knowledge of effective comparison/contrast techniques as presented in

Chapter Four. Then write your own opinion of the topic in another paragraph. You may refer to the authors' ideas to support your opinion.

Dear Editor:

Much has been written about the changing roles of women in society in recent years. Women in the U.S. presently hold such high political offices as Supreme Court Justice; they are being promoted rapidly in businesses so that the companies can advertise their "equal opportunity" pledges; women are in the majority as students at many colleges and universities; they are being promoted to the highest ranks in the armed services. Women are becoming increasingly career oriented; in fact, many women today view their professions as the single most important aspect of their lives. However, let us not forget how much the nation is sacrificing to women's career ambitions.

The obvious first victim of the women's movement is the family. Children are left with baby-sitters or day-care personnel for ten to twelve hours a day. During the Gulf War crisis, children whose parents were both soldiers serving on active duty were abandoned to neighbors or relatives. In fact, pregnancy, signaling the arrival of sons and daughters, often results in consternation and fear rather than joy and fulfillment for the prospective parents. The pressures of full-time employment have led to the break-up of millions of families, resulting in even less parent-child contact than before. Divorce courts are filled to overflowing and the taxpayers' money is spent endlessly in courts' attempts to obtain child-support payments from unwilling fathers and even mothers. Our society was built upon the foundations of a strong family life; changing women's roles have threatened the very existence of family and the values only a strong family can instill.

A second victim of the women's movement is perhaps less obvious but, in the long run, potentially more destructive: the mental and physical health of our citizens. Women, who had previously been protected from such awesome killers as hypertension and heart disease find themselves increasingly susceptible to these illnesses. The difference between the life expectancies of U.S. males and females has been a large one: on the average, American women are expected to live about six years longer than men. However, the stresses of career-oriented lives are narrowing that gap. Add to that the potential for an increased death rate that can be expected if women are allowed to take active combat roles in future military operations. In addition, both men and women are experiencing more mental health problems than ever before; mental health clinics and psychiatric wards are bulging with people who have not been able to cope with the changing expectations placed on the two sexes by modern society.

Let us return to the days when a man was a man and a woman knew her place, when Dad brought home the bacon and Mom fried it. Children were happier, families were stronger, and people were healthier. We don't need Sandra Day O'Connor sitting at the Supreme Court bench; we need Mother standing at the door to welcome the children home. If the American people don't wake up and recognize what is happening to our nation, all those billions of defense dollars will be wasted. There will be no country to defend.

John Q. Wonder

Dear Editor:

Regarding the rhetoric of the anti-feminist forces, I would like to add a few words of common sense to the millions of sentences published about the subject. Reason has often been thrown out the window in favor of emotional references to "Mom" and "apple pie." An enlightened person today must realize that a better symbol for the American family today is "Mom and Dad" and "carpools." This does not mean that we have abandoned something good in favor of a worse situation. In fact, many people would rather be living in our modern, progressive age than at any other time in history. Equal rights for women should be considered inherent, not earned. Our God-given right to be treated equally in society has finally been recognized, not won.

Opponents of the now defunct Equal Rights Amendment entertained some kind of vague, Victorian notion that women were born to be cooks and housekeepers. Would anyone assert that men were born to be firemen or truck drivers? Nonsense! Homemaking is a career choice just as engineering, medicine, and business are. I have no argument with or criticism of any woman who consciously chooses this field as a career, but I vehemently oppose any forcing of this decision. If men want apple pie, *The Joy of Cooking* has a wonderful, fool-proof recipe that even they can follow!

It has been suggested that the women's movement is responsible for the breakdown of the American family. It is true that there are a great many more divorces today than there were before World War II and that many women who would have stayed in unhappy home situations years ago are much quicker to leave today. But does this mean the family is weaker? Perhaps many unhappy women stayed in bad marriages in the past because they had no means of support away from their husbands, but does this mean family life was good? Remember, too, that women whose husbands abandoned them in the past were objects of pity to the society around them because they were often plunged into poverty and forced to seek low-paying jobs. If they had received educations and career training in their youth, they wouldn't have had such tragic fates. No self-respecting woman of today would allow herself to be placed in such a humiliating situation.

By sharing the responsibility for the welfare and economic security of the family with their husbands, today's wives can actually help build stronger, happier families. Men who once had to shoulder the family burden entirely alone may find their stress lessened and their health better than before. Men may even start to live longer, which means there will be fewer lonely widows in the future. How could such a positive conse-quence of the equal rights movement be ignored by so-called enlightened opponents?

The little girls of today can look forward to a future of equality and shared responsibility with men, and the little boys should be glad of it. Reason must prevail in this debate. The future of our nation depends upon the intelligence and strength of all of its people, not of the male half only. It is time everyone recognized this fact.

Jane P. Marvel

Exercise 3. Summarizing for Argumentation   III

Discuss the following article with your class. Then summarize it and write a paragraph in which you give your personal reaction to it. Do you feel you are like "Contradiction Man"? In what ways? How are you dif-ferent? What does this opinion article say about human nature? (Terms marked with an asterisk are explained at the end of the article.)

Contradiction Man

Contradiction Man is in his car. He is in a hurry and irritable. He whizzes around one of Washington's wonderful traffic circles, a veritable "Charge of the Light Brigade"*—cars to the right of him, cars to the left of him, volley and thunder—and pedestrians keep walking against the light. Contradiction Man hates jaywalkers, and so he pretends to keep coming, to not see them. Of course, he does see them, and he can stop on a dime, but he shows by his actions that he is not a driver to be trifled with. Contradiction Man pulls into a parking garage, sure he has set some people right.

Now Contradiction Man has to get across the street. He is in the mid-dle of the block. He looks three ways: at cars coming in either direction and for cops. The coast is clear. Contradiction Man starts to walk across. Oops, a car's coming. Contradiction Man does a Wallenda* on the double yellow line. He sways one way and then another, working, as it were, without a net. More cars come. Contradiction Man makes himself as thin as possible and thinks that this might be IT*. He curses the cars. Why won't they give him a break?

Who is Contradiction Man? He is me. Maybe, just maybe, he is you too. He is the personification of human nature. He believes, wholeheart-edly and without reservation, that out of sight is out of mind. He also believes, wholeheartedly and without reservation, that absence makes the heart grow fonder. Contradiction Man believes in both sides of the nature versus nurture controversy. Education can make all the difference, but, let's face it, some people just are the way they are. His grandmother was right about that, but then again, she knew almost nothing.

Contradiction Man is back in the car. A bicyclist is up ahead. Contradiction Man hates bikers. He finds it hard to gauge their speed and how far ahead they may be. He thinks they should not be allowed to take an entire lane on a street, and he is always anxious that one of them may veer suddenly into the path of the car. Contradiction Man would like to see bikes banned from the city streets.

Now Contradiction Man is on his bike. He has a brand-new red one, a mountain bike that, God willing, will never see the mountains. The bike has 18 gears, at least 10 of which he will never use. No matter, Contradiction Man loves his bike and, indeed, loves to bike. He is, though, a most unpredictable biker. He sometimes veers out into traffic, often to avoid a pothole or something. He uses the city streets. He can feel the sheer hatred of drivers, like sun on his back. Contradiction Man does not care. He is entitled to the road. Read the law, fella.

Most of the time, though, Contradiction Man hates bikers. And most of all, he hates couriers*. They are a true menace. They weave in and out of traffic and come roaring down the sidewalk. Contradiction Man fears them and entertains fantasies of knocking them off their bikes as they whiz down the sidewalk. On the other hand, Contradiction Man also uses these couriers. When he does, he is grateful for their speed and their sheer recklessness, and when the package arrives, he never asks how many lives were lost in the process. With the arrival of the package, Contradiction Man returns to his original state of hatred.

Contradiction Man is an ecologist. He loves trees and all things green and even some that are blue, like the sky. He wants everyone to protect the environment, and he would, if he could, reserve capital punishment for littering. Yet Contradiction Man has no time to sort his trash. He feels strongly that he should be excepted from this requirement since he is always busy. Others may sort their trash. In fact, they should be forced to. Contradiction Man relies on them for a clean environment.

Contradiction Man believes wholeheartedly in the public schools. They are where he was educated, and he is convinced they are essential to democracy. Nevertheless, Contradiction Man sends his children to private schools because he believes they provide a better education. On this particular issue, Contradiction Man feels strongly—both ways.

Contradiction Man believes in Old-Fashioned Values. But not for himself. He believes firmly in teaching the classics, but he has never had time to read them himself. He is opposed to abortion, but not if someone he loves needs one, and he believes that the people are always right, except when they disagree with him.

Contradiction Man weeps for a White Christmas but hates snow. He is irate at how cows are mistreated to produce veal, but, boy, does he love a good grilled chop—medium rare, thank you. Contradiction Man believes wholeheartedly in the pernicious effects of cholesterol, but not when it comes in the form of a good steak. He knows he should diet, but then diets don't work. He should exercise more, but Winston Churchill didn't and Jim Fixx* did. At any rate, Contradiction Man believes doctors know nothing except, of course, for the ones who cure him. As for lawyers, they are a noble lot and also a bunch of shysters. The press is irresponsible, but without it we are doomed, and the First Amendment protects everything written, except articles about me or my friends.

Contradiction Man might be confused with a hypocrite. Nothing could be further from the truth. Contradiction Man believes sincerely in what he espouses at the time he espouses it. He has contempt for someone who says one thing and does another. Unless, of course...

by Richard Cohen in his column
"Critic at Large"
©1991, Washington Post Writers Group. Reprinted with permission.

glossary

"Charge of the Light Brigade"—famous epic poem by Tennyson about a battle in the Crimean War

does a Wallenda—performs a tightrope walking act (Wallenda was a famous circus performer)

IT—end of his life

couriers—messengers who make their deliveries by bicycle in large cities in the U.S.

Jim Fixx—famous runner and author who died of a heart attack he suffered while running

Exercise 4. Summarizing for Argumentation IV

Write a summary of the article on page 176, "Education Benefits for Illegals?" by Ralph P. Anderson. Save your summary for a later writing assignment.

WRITING ASSIGNMENT ONE:

Writing an Argument Together

Work in a group of four or five to discuss and analyze the following opinion article. The author, George Will, mentions many famous Americans in his article. Many of them will be familiar to the members of your group, and many others are described by the context of the article. However, you will need to do some research on those names mentioned that you cannot identify.

Of Money and Men

From Britain comes the germ of a good idea. The Duke of Wellington's picture is being replaced on the five-pound note by that of George Stephenson, the engineer who developed steam power. Michael Faraday, the physicist (electrical induction), is replacing Shakespeare on the 20-pound note.

There is proper indignation about the demotion of Shakespeare, the greatest shaper of that nation's discourse and imagination. But science and technology deserve honors. A British intellectual says sniffily that although Stephenson is "a man of eminence" he "hardly serves to fill you with patriotic fervor." Well, even if making us fervid is government's proper business, why celebrate so many political figures, such as the Duke? Wellington deserves his ample honors for squishing Napoleon. But what good is done by reminding people, redundantly, of the glories of their most famous political and military pinups? Better they should be nudged to note that science, commerce and the arts are national glories, and necessities, too. Actually, the British know this. Florence Nightingale and Sir Christopher Wren, the architect, adorn some paper notes.

Many European nations steer clear of political persons on their paper currency, partly because those nations are so old and grumpy no one can praise any political figure from their past without picking a fight. German currency features poets, musicians, scientists and the like, or portraits of unknown people by famous painters (Durer, Cranach). That is understandable. If our political history were like Germany's, we, too, would dodge the subject. In France, where governance is emphatically not the nation's *gloire,* the currency features cultural heroes such as Pascal, Montesquieu, Delacroix, Debussy. Italians, who regard their government as a disagreeable rumor or a temporary inconvenience, decorate their currency with portraits of some of those who have helped decorate and ennoble their peninsula: Maria Montessori, educator and physician; composer Bellini; Bernini, sculptor and architect. The painter Caravaggio is on the 100,000-lira note, worth about $79.

Until 1969, when bills larger than $100 were withdrawn, 11 political men had their portraits on U.S. paper currency: Washington ($1), Jefferson ($2), Lincoln ($5), Hamilton ($10), Jackson ($20), Grant ($50), Franklin ($100), McKinley ($500), Cleveland ($1,000), Madison ($5,000), Chase ($10,000). Now, it does not matter that most Americans haven't a clue who Chase was (Lincoln's first Treasury Secretary). It matters more, but not much, that the sainted Madison, our subtlest political thinker, was relegated to rare appearances on a large denomination. However, what is seriously wrong with the list is its monomania. Politicians are not the sole sources of a nation's success and grandeur.

There is much more to national enrichment, material and moral, than the people who make its laws and run its institutions of governance. Those important things depend on other things—habits, mores, customs, values, virtues—that are shaped, vivified, nurtured and husbanded by people often working far from the public arena.

So, to tutor the nation in the myriad sources of its greatness, let's scrub all the political people from the greenbacks. And while we're at it, let's get rid of the green, which is intensely boring. Let's reissue the big bills and liven up the currency with many colors and the following faces:

$1: Mark Twain. The smaller the denomination, the more common the usage. Who deserves this place more than the man who, through Huck Finn, put the American language of common usage into literature?

$2 (Let's print more of these, please—they are so convenient, and not just at the racetrack): For our jazzier money, let's have someone representing our distinctive music, jazz and the musical stage—Scott Joplin, W.C. Handy, Louis Armstrong, Duke Ellington, George Gershwin.

$5: Choose a painter for the prettified currency, perhaps Mary Cassatt, or Sargent, Remington, Whistler, Homer.

$10: Someone who exemplifies the American turn of the mind—Emerson or William James.

$20: Alexander Joy Cartwright, who codified the great game, or Willie Mays, who perfected it.

$50: America's inventors democratized science, turning technology to common uses, so pick one: Fulton, Whitney, Edison or the Wright brothers.

$100: One source of America's success is public education. Therefore: Horace Mann.

$500: By the written word, especially novels, America emancipated itself culturally from the Old World. So make room for Hawthorne, Melville, Wharton, Fitzgerald, Hemingway or Faulkner.

$1,000: If money is, as Emerson said, the prose of life, let's put a poet on it, Emily Dickinson or Walt Whitman.

$5,000: Henry Ford (or Charles Kettering or Alfred Sloan). A giant of American industry, a pioneer of mass manufacturing, should grace a large denomination.

$10,000: Wealth without wisdom is not merely barren, it is a menace. Therefore here, at the pinnacle of the currency that is supposed to serve as a store of value, is the place for philosophy in the form of a man who is not much read anymore, which is our loss: John Dewey.

It is frustrating having so many eligible people and so few denominations of paper currency. Of course, there is no reason why we could not rotate the people portrayed on the paper money. The government constantly changes the value of the currency (always in one direction: down), so the paper could be redecorated periodically. The paper currency could be a slowly expanding honors system—sort of a House of Lords for the eminent departed. Someday—not soon, let us hope—we shall want to make room for, say, some American writers still writing. What fun it would be one day to whip out a wallet and pay for dinner with two Eudora Weltys, three Peter Taylors and a Saul Bellow.

Furthermore, we may not always have just 11 denominations. By the time our government gets done debauching our currency (actually, government's inflationary work is never done), we may be buying loaves of bread with $10,000 bills. We will need bigger denominations, so save the names of those (Frank Lloyd Wright, Aaron Copland, James Fenimore Cooper, Robert Frost, Michael Jordan...) who do not make our new varsity 11.

George F. Will
Newsweek, June 3, 1991

1. *Do research.* With your group, write a list of the names you need to identify. Then divide the list into equal numbers to assign to each member of your group. At your next class meeting, each group member must be able to tell the group about the persons on whom he or she has done research. In carrying out your research, you may ask native-born Americans, consult unabridged dictionaries or encyclopedias, or ask a librarian for assistance.

2. *Discuss the arguments.* After you have identified the Americans mentioned, discuss with your group the proposal that George Will makes. Is it practical? Is it worth the time and money it would entail? What people are portrayed on currency in your own country? What colors are used on bills? Are there other names you would include in Will's suggested list? As a group, come to a consensus on the issue. Write a list of reasons why you support or disagree with the proposal.

3. *Write an essay.* Each of you will take the list and use it to write, in essay form, your reaction to the article. *Remember to include a summary of the George Will article before you give your personal reaction to it.*

4. *Revise your essay.* Share your essay with the others in your group. Look for adequate support for your argument in your partners' essays, as they will do in yours. Have you made a strong enough case to support your opinion? Have you anticipated counterarguments and refuted them?

5. *Edit your essay.* Edit for errors in spelling, punctuation, grammar, and sentence structure before turning your final draft in to the teacher.

WRITING ASSIGNMENT TWO:
Writing an Argument on Your Own

Refute the essay on the education of illegal immigrants which you summarized in Exercise 4. Include your summary in your essay. Be sure to examine the points the author makes in the original essay and formulate a response to each one. Write your reaction in essay form. Follow the usual steps for revising and editing for errors in spelling, punctuation, grammar, and sentence structure.

FINAL WRITING ASSIGNMENT:

Independent Writing

It is time to synthesize all that you have learned about writing an essay. In this final assignment, you will use facts and statistics to support your opinion on one of the following topics. In order to do this, you will need to do research on the topic in the library and summarize the information that you find. Be sure your statistics are accurate, relevant, and documented. You may need to analyze charts and graphs to gather appropriate facts to support your argument.

After you have finished your research, follow the steps in the writing process that are the most appropriate to your own style. Brainstorm with a classmate if you have found that to be a useful technique. In planning the organization of your first draft, take notes and develop an outline if that has been a step that you have found to be helpful. Then write an essay in which you use the information you have gathered to reinforce your arguments. In the revision stage, you might want to ask someone else to read your draft to check that you have sufficient supporting details, that the information you have included is relevant to your topic, and that you have anticipated any possible counterarguments and adequately refuted them.

In the final stage, be sure to edit your essay before turning it in to your teacher. Look with a critical eye at the sentence forms you have used. Is there variety of forms? Have you used appropriate sentence-combining techniques? Do you use parallel structures? Make sure to edit for spelling and punctuation errors as well.

Topics:

1. The value of a college education in terms of salaries earned by college graduates versus high school graduates.
2. The effect of driver's training on the safety records of teen-aged drivers.
3. The importance of the labor union movement in terms of salaries and benefits to workers.
4. The effectiveness of burglar alarms to protect private residences.
5. 176

6. Implications of computerization on the job market.
7. The effects of seat belt use in saving lives of people involved in traffic accidents.
8. The impact of second-hand smoke on the health of people who work in close contact with smokers.
9. Your choice. (Supplied by you or your teacher)

APPENDIX I

Review of Sentence Punctuation

The punctuation items presented in this review have been introduced in various chapters of the text. For a more comprehensive list of punctuation rules, consult a modern text of English grammar and usage.

The Period

1. Use a period at the end of a statement, command, or request:

   Parks provide a necessary relief from the asphalt and buildings of a city.

   Sign your name on the line.

   Please give me your opinion about this matter.

The Comma

1. Use a comma to separate words or phrases in a series:

   Most students at this university major in engineering, social sciences, or health sciences.

   Positions in this firm differ in the training required, the opportunities for advancement, and the salaries offered.

   • Do not use a comma when only two items are joined by *and*.

   Reading and writing are equally important language skills.

2. Use commas to set off words in apposition:

   Lydia Schurman, a professor of English literature, recently published her first novel.

3. Use a comma between two independent sentences joined by a coordinating word:

   We have worked on this project for a long time, and I am glad it is almost finished.

   • Do not use a comma to join an independent sentence and a verb phrase.

   Pat finished studying for the exam and went to bed early.

4. Use commas to set off a nonessential adjective clause:

   Professor Conerly, who had taught at the college for over 25 years, finally retired and moved to Mississippi.

   Route 7, which connects Alexandria and Leesburg, is one of Northern Virginia's busiest highways.

   • Do not use a comma to set off an essential adjective clause.

There were two professors. The professor who had taught at the college for over 25 years finally retired and moved to Mississippi. The other one did not.

The road that connects Alexandria and Leesburg is one of Northern Virginia's busiest highways.

5. Use a comma after a dependent adverbial clause at the beginning of a sentence:

Before Marilyn accepted a job teaching English in Poland, she had many years of experience in both the United States and Asia.

If you ever have a chance to visit the United States, be sure to include the Southwest on your itinerary.

• Do not generally use a comma when the dependent clause follows the main clause.

Dr. Selinger realized that he would never finish his project if he didn't work on it every weekend.

6. Use a comma to set off long participial phrases preceding an independent clause:

Realizing the need for more income for his family, John took on a part-time evening job in a restaurant.

Having rewritten the research paper twice, the student refused to revise it one more time.

7. Use a comma to set off sentence connectors:

The school children were not doing well on national standardized exams. Therefore, the superintendent decided to take drastic measures.

Mr. and Mrs. May really wanted to take a vacation. However, they never seemed to be able to save enough money.

Most of the people in the community were in favor of the group home for handicapped people. They didn't, however, want it in their own neighborhood.

8. Use a comma in sentences with direct quotations:

"That's the last time I'll accept late papers," said the frustrated teacher.

The doctor warned, "You'd better stop smoking if you want to live a long life."

The Semicolon

Use a semicolon in place of a period to separate independent clauses joined by logical connectors, such as *however, moreover, therefore, consequently*. Follow these words with a comma (see number 7 preceding):

The forms of the verbs are very important in your mastery of English; therefore, you should memorize them.

A better diet will help you to feel more energetic; moreover, it will probably help you to live longer.

Quotation Marks

Use double quotation marks to enclose a direct quotation:

Gail said, "Let's go out for lunch."

The lawyer asked, "Why do you want to sue your friend?"

•Do not use quotation marks in indirect speech.

The lawyer asked him why he wanted to sue his friend.

APPENDIX 2

Summary of Connecting Words

	Conjunctions	Logical Connectors	Adverbial Expressions
Addition	and	also, besides in addition moreover	
Contrast/ concession	but yet	however nevertheless on the other hand	although though even though while
Choice or alternative	or nor	otherwise	
Result/ purpose	so	therefore thus accordingly as a result for this reason consequently	so (that) in order (that)
Restatement		in short in effect in other words	
Restatement to intensify		in fact indeed as a matter of fact indeed	
Cause	for		because since
Condition			if, unless as long as provided (that)
Time			when, before, after, since, as, while, until
Manner			as if as though
Place			where, wherever

APPENDIX 3

Computers and the Writing Process

Revising and editing are time-consuming tasks that are unwelcome to most writers. Revising with a paper and pencil means starting over and recopying many times. Using the word processing capabilities of the computer makes the writing process much easier and reduces the amount of time spent on the process. What are some of the benefits of using the computer for writing?

1. *Computers can be used to generate and store ideas for later use.* In the early stages of thinking, ideas can be typed in for safe-keeping using a variety of techniques. These ideas can be developed into essays later.

2. *Computers allow easy revision and rewriting.* Once text is entered, it can be easily moved, copied, and rearranged. Words, phrases, sentences, paragraphs, and even whole pages can be inserted or deleted anywhere in the text.

3. *Computers allow easy editing.* Punctuation is easily changed. Spelling can be checked using a spell-checker.

4. *Collaborative writing is more easily done on a computer.* Because all students in a group (usually not more than three) can see the screen, collaborative writing becomes more workable. Students feel much more a part of the collaborative effort, become more involved in what is being written, and find it harder to sit back and let someone else do the work.

5. *Writing produced on a computer has a professional look.* Teachers often downgrade students with poor handwriting because they cannot read what they say. Writing on the computer has distinct benefits for students whose native language alphabets differ from that of English.

6. *Writing on a computer has become a necessary skill, and it can be fun.* Many jobs these days, even those that are not directly related to computers (such as computer programming) require computer skills. Using and learning about modern technology can be exciting as well as rewarding.

What do you need to know first?

The computer used as a word processor is a revolutionary tool for writing. We must remember, however, that it is not a glorified typewriter. It is not just for typing in a text once it is written on paper. If we use it that way, we are not using one of its major advantages, its capabilities for revision. Writing activities done on the computer can actively support and promote the steps in the writing process: brainstorming, planning, revising, and editing.

What do you need to know before you begin to write on the computer?

1. *Learn the basic operating system of the computer you will use.* Before you begin using the computer for writing, you will need to know how to use the software, boot the system, prepare disks, and load and run the word processing program. You will also need to learn how to save text, name files, load files, clear the screen, and use the file directory.

2. *Learn how to enter text.* The word processor makes entering text easy. All the material you type is stored on data disks. You can return to the text at any time to revise and fix errors. Even people who use the "hunt and peck" method of typing find that they can use the word processor. If you don't know how to type, most computer writing labs have access to a typing tutor. These computer programs can teach you to type directly on the screen and can also help you increase your typing speed.

3. *Learn how to make changes and save your text.* Once you have entered text, you can make a variety of changes. You need to know how to move the cursor through text, scroll up and down, insert text, erase, block and move material, and reformat. After you have made changes, you will need to save your changes.

4. *Learn how to print.* One of the best things about writing on a computer is that you can print your copy at any time to see how it looks. Most writers use this "hard copy" to review what they have written and plan for the next revision.

Your teacher or computer writing lab coordinator can help you learn to use the word processing program in your lab. Some labs have tutorial programs that will also be useful.

How can computers be used in the writing process?

Once you have the basic skills for using a computer, you can use it to make the writing process easier. Here are some suggested strategies:

1. *Use a computer for gathering ideas (brainstorming).* Once you have a topic to write about, you need to begin getting your ideas down even though you may not have developed a thesis yet.

   ■ *List ideas.* Begin putting down ideas in sentences or groups of sentences. Hit the return or enter key at the end of each idea group. Don't worry about any order. Just get your ideas down.

- *Create an idea or "freewriting" draft.* Have a clear screen. Allow yourself a block of time to write, and let yourself follow your thoughts wherever they may lead. Don't stop to judge your ideas for quality, logic, or relevance. Write as much as you can until you have exhausted all of your ideas.

- *Turn off the monitor.* Write ideas without seeing what you write. (This method works well for writers who have trouble getting started because they worry about making mistakes.)

2. *Use a computer to help you plan and organize.* There are several ways the computer can help you to plan. The way you choose depends on your personal preference.

   - *Organize your list.* Use the "move" feature of your program to block and move your groups of sentences. Perhaps you have printed out a hard copy first. Read through and number the blocks. Then return to the computer and use the move function to reorganize them. Continue this process until your ideas are in order.

   - *Analyze your draft for ideas.* With a pencil, go over a printout of your "freewriting" draft to find major ideas that stand out. Mark ideas that you want to focus on. Identify places that need further explanation. Look for examples that support your ideas. Delete ideas that seem unrelated. Use your analysis to begin creating a writing plan.

   - *Begin to focus.* Generating a list or a draft and putting the ideas in order often lead to a clearer focus. Look over your list or draft. Before you develop your writing plan further, write your purpose for writing and your thesis statement at the beginning of the file. You may find that your thesis has emerged.

   - *Use an outline.* Some writers prefer not to use the list or draft for generating ideas. They would rather begin with a formal outline, with all the ideas numbered and ordered. An outline can be very useful when the topic is large and complex. The computer can help. Some word processing programs (WordPerfect, for example) have a built-in outline template to help writers produce a working outline. Such outline or "idea generating" programs can also be bought separately. They use a series of questions to help the writer think about a topic. They then arrange the material into an outline. (See also Chapter Three of the text.)

3. *Use a computer to write your first draft.* With your list, freewriting, or outline in front of you, begin to write. Much as you did with your freewriting, write quickly to get as much down as you can, but this time follow your plan.

4. *Use the computer's revision capabilities.* After you have written a draft, print a hard copy. Read over your copy with a careful eye for the organization and logic of your ideas. Go back to the computer and use the block and move functions to move paragraphs or blocks of text. Add and delete sentences as necessary.

5. *Use the computer's editing capabilities.* Use your computer's spell-checker to check spelling. Then edit your paper. Many writers find it difficult to edit from the computer screen. Print a hard copy once again. This time use a keen eye to check for other surface errors, such as punctuation, subject-verb agreement, and any other specific problem you know you need to pay attention to.

INDEX

CREDITS

We would like to thank the authors, photographers, and holders of copyright for use of the following material.

Text

Page 112, Figure 4.1: Disclaimer: TOEFL pie chart selected from the TOEFL "Program News," Educational Testing Service, Fall, 1990. Permission to reprint TOEFL test material does not constitute review or endorsement by Educational Testing Service of this publication as a whole or of any other testing information it may contain.

Pages 191–192: Curt Suplee, "Robo-Roads: Making Highways Smart" (adaptation), *The Washington Post*, May 27, 1991, p. A3.

Pages 195–197: Richard Cohen, "Critic at Large" (column), ©1991, Washington Post Writers Group. Reprinted with permission.

Photos

Carolou Marquet/Northern Virginia Community College: pp. 1, 20, 27, 95, 124, 137, 156, 173

Elizabeth Crews/Stock, Boston: p. 55

Spencer Grant/Stock, Boston: p. 123

Hung Pham/Northern Virginia Community College: p. 67

Reuters/Bettmann, p. 198